the good goodbye

THE TRANSFORMATIVE POWER OF CONVERSATION AT THE END OF LIFE

MAUREEN P. KEELEY, PH.D.

JULIE M. YINGLING, PH.D.

HAY HOUSE

HAY HOUSE INDIA
New Delhi • London • Sydney
Carlsbad, California • New York City

Hay House Publishers (India) Pvt Ltd
Muskaan Complex, Plot No. 3, B-2, Vasant Kunj, New Delhi – 110070, India

Hay House LLC, P.O. Box 5100, Carlsbad, CA 92018-5100, USA
Hay House UK Ltd, 1st Floor, Crawford Corner, 91-93 Baker Street, London W1U 6QQ, UK
Hay House Australia Publishing Pty Ltd, 18/36 Ralph St., Alexandria NSW 2015, Australia

Email: contact@hayhouse.co.in
Website: www.hayhouse.co.in

Cover design: Karla Schweer
Interior design: Joe Bernier

First published by Hay House India, 2025
10 9 8 7 6 5 4 3 2 1

ISBN 978-93-6611-483-5

Printed at Repro India Limited

MIX
Paper from responsible sources
FSC
www.fsc.org
FSC® C047271

Hay House is committed to a sustainable future for our business, our readers and our planet. This book is made from Forest Stewardship Council® certified paper.

Praise for *The Good Goodbye*

"This compassionate and gentle read offers invaluable guidance for navigating end-of-life conversations with loved ones. Through heartfelt stories, it helps ease the fear and uncertainty that often accompany this delicate time. Speak from the heart with those you cherish, and let this book be a gift—not only for them but for yourself as well."

— **Beth Leconte**, executive director, Osher Lifelong Learning Institute, University of Rhode Island

"An important book on a much-needed subject."

— **Bronnie Ware**, author of *The Top Five Regrets of the Dying*

"An invaluable guide for the most poignant moment each of us will face in life—the death of a loved one. With insight illuminated by years of studying end-of-life conversations, the authors present practical wisdom for making the final goodbye a time imbued with love and grace. This beautifully written book, interwoven with the stories of those who have experienced final conversations with loved ones, offers comfort to the dying and hope for the living."

— **Steven A. Beebe, Ph.D.**, Regents' and University Distinguished Professor Emeritus, past president, National Communication Association

"The Good Goodbye *could not be timelier. In a culture terrified of death, it is refreshing to hear stories about the power of connection and communication at the end of life. This book has the potential to truly change lives and relationships."*

— **Dr. Mark Generous**, associate professor, Department of Communication, California State Polytechnic University, Pomona

"Maureen and Julie have created an educational and inspiring resource to open our hearts and minds to the many gifts of final communications with our loved ones. These shared words and messages will help us and our loved ones to live presently, to communicate openly and beyond words, and to die peacefully. The conversations, summaries, and tips provide insight, comfort, and helpful discussion starters to help us, at all ages, have a good goodbye."

— **Kathy O'Neel Webster**, certified death doula

"Every day is a gift and a challenge when supporting the Dying. These authors have shared stories, conversations, and helpful tips from the Living who have experienced living with the Dying. This book is a must-read for anyone caring for or supporting a dying relative, friend, or patient."

— **MJ Henderson, MS, RN, GNP-BC (retired)**,
gerontological nursing consultant

For all the generous people who shared their final conversations with us and taught us about the good goodbye

CONTENTS

Notes on Terminology xv
Acknowledgments xvii

PART ONE: UNDERSTANDING FINAL CONVERSATIONS

Chapter 1: Finding the Good in Goodbye 3

Final Conversations That Transform Us 4
- What Are Final Conversations? 4
- Transformation 4

The Surprising Gifts That Come from Final Conversations 4
- Gifts for the Dying 5
- Gifts for the Living 5

Fear of Death and Dying 6
- Fear of the Unknown 6
- Fear of the Pain of Loss 6

What Will You Find Here? 7
- Real Stories from Real People 7
- Advice from Communication Experts 7

How to Use This Book 8
- Find What You Need 8
- Enjoy the Stories 8

Chapter 2: What's Culture Got to Do with It? 9

Cultural Beliefs About Death and Dying 9
- The Role of Death in Life: Avoidance or Acceptance 10
- Death Is the Enemy: We Avoid It 10
- Death Is a Natural Part of Life: We Accept It 11
  - Family Norms 11
  - Cultural Effects 12
  - Mixed Messages 12

Communication About Death: Silence or Openness 13
- Silence and Secrets 13
  - Family Norms 13
  - Cultural Effects 13
  - Mixed Messages 14

Open, Honest Talks ... 16
Family Norms ... 16
Cultural Effects ... 16
Mixed Messages ... 17

Company at the End: Alone or Together ... 17
Dying in Isolation ... 17
Dying in Close Relationship ... 18

SUMMARY ... 19
TRADITIONAL ... 19
STANDARD AMERICAN ... 19
EMERGENT ... 20
TIPS FOR BETTER CONVERSATIONS ... 20

Chapter 3: Beyond Words: Nonverbal Messages ... 23

See Me; Feel Me; Hear Me; Touch Me ... 24
Eyes: Windows to the Soul ... 24
Face Reveals Emotion; Body Conveys the Intensity of the Emotion ... 25
Voice: Sounds from the Heart ... 27
Touch: Ways to Connect and to Let Go ... 27

Proximity and Time Communicate Closeness ... 29
Proximity: Being Nearby Simply Feels Better ... 29
Time Matters ... 30

The Importance of "Stuff" ... 31
Tokens: A Little Something ... 31
Symbolic Possessions: Perfect Beds and Canned Peaches ... 32

Revelations Through Smell and Physical Appearance ... 33
Scents Can Soothe, Aggravate, or Reveal ... 33
Physical Appearance Reveals ... 34

SUMMARY ... 34
TIPS FOR BETTER CONVERSATIONS ... 35

PART TWO: FINAL CONVERSATION THEMES

Chapter 4: I Love You ... 39

Loving the Dying in Intimate Relationships ... 40
Giving and Receiving Direct Messages of Love ... 40
Completing the Relationship, Moving Forward ... 42

Perception Is Reality When It Comes to Love ... 42

Finally, Love Expressed 44
Love Spoken for the First Time 44
As All Else Fades . . . Love Becomes All 45
Nothing More to Say: A Good Goodbye 47
SUMMARY 48
TIPS FOR BETTER CONVERSATIONS 49

Chapter 5: Everyday Talk 51
I'm Not Dead Yet! Continuing the Relationship to the End 51
Small Talk, Pleasantries, and Simple Joys 53
Shared Interests and Activities 55
Routine Interactions, Shared Rituals, and Private Codes 56
Preserving the Relationship for the Future: Shared Memories 57
Challenges with Everyday Talk 59
Avoiding Difficult Conversations 59
Coping with Negativity 60
Gifts from Everyday Talk 61
Cementing the Bond 61
Lightening the Load 61
SUMMARY 62
TIPS FOR BETTER CONVERSATIONS 63

Chapter 6: Taking Care of the Business of Death and Dying 65
Ask Them What Their Wishes Are . . . If They Haven't Already Told You 66
Legal End-of-Life Documents 66
Informal, Nonbinding End-of-Life Conversations 67
Honest Talk About Death and Dying 67
When It's Time for Hospice 69
Memorial Wishes 71
No Weeping Angels 72
Please Wear White (and Other Instructions) 73
Housekeeping: To-Do Lists 73
SUMMARY 75
TIPS FOR BETTER CONVERSATIONS 76

Chapter 7: What I Know About You and Why You Want to Know It 79

How the Dying Changes Your View of Yourself 80
- Strengths and Talents: The Mirror the Dying Holds for the Living 80
- Affirmations: Loving Yourself as the Dying Loved You 81
- Advice from the Dying: Words to Grow On 82

Maturing a Self: Seeing Through Their Eyes 84
- What Would They Do? 85
- What Would They Say? 85
- Seeing Myself Through Their Eyes 85

Switching Roles with the Dying: "Who's the Parent Now?" 86
- I Became the Parent 86
- She Didn't Have to Be My Mother Anymore 87

Accepting Self and Pursuing Life 87
- Confirmation of Your Beliefs 87
- Change in Direction 87

SUMMARY 88
TIPS FOR BETTER CONVERSATIONS 88

Chapter 8: Grace Happens: Spiritual Messages 91

Witnessing Faith 92
- Testimony from the Dying 92
- Testimony from the Living 92
- Prayers and Hymns at the End of Life 94

Experiencing Spirit 95
- The Spiritual Experiences of the Dying 95
- The Spiritual Experiences of the Living 97
- Images of Heaven 99
- Messages and Whispers from Angels and Guides 100

SUMMARY 101
TIPS FOR BETTER CONVERSATIONS 101

Chapter 9: Healing Damaged Relationships 103

Releasing the Negativity 104
- Being the Adult to Clean Up the Damage 104
- Stop the Blame Game 107

Letting Go of What You Cannot Control....107
Acknowledging and Forgiving....107
Acceptance of One Another's Differences....109
Creating a New Kind of Relationship with the Dying....110
Receiving the Surprise Apology....110
Closing a Door, Opening a Window....112
Don't Make It Worse: Make Your Peace....113
SUMMARY....114
TIPS FOR BETTER CONVERSATIONS....115

PART THREE: TRANSFORMATIONAL EFFECTS OF FINAL CONVERSATIONS

Chapter 10: Benefits of Final Conversations....119
Acceptance....120
Recognition and Release of Pain for the Dying....120
The Dying's Acceptance of Their Impending Death....120
Closure....121
Nothing Left Unsaid....121
Closure Takes Time....122
Coping....122
No Regrets....123
Vulnerability....124
Witnessing the Dying's Peace....124
Personal Growth....124
Relating to Others....125
New Possibilities....125
Personal Strength....126
Spiritual Change....127
Appreciation for Life....128
SUMMARY....129
TIPS FOR BETTER CONVERSATIONS....130

Chapter 11: Out of the Mouth of Babes: Children Talk About Their Final Conversations....131
Children Tell Us How to Say Goodbye....131

Talking with the Dying Throughout Childhood 132
Preschool (4–6 years old) 132
Grammar School (7–11 years old) 133
Openness 134
Family Rituals 134
Tweens and Teens (12–18 years old) 134
Openness 135
Love Gifts 135

Advice from Kids to Kids and for Kids 135
Advice for Kids Facing the Death of a Loved One 136
Affirm Your Relationship: Spend the Time, Reveal Yourself, Show Your Love, Be There 136
Be Strong; Stay Positive 137
Talk to Supportive Adults; Find Your Trusted Others 138
Advice for the Dying When Interacting with Kids 138
Affirm Your Relationship: Tell Your Story 138
Be Truthful and Honest; Be Real 139
Show What You Know About Them 140

SUMMARY 141
TIPS FOR BETTER CONVERSATIONS 141

Chapter 12: Growing Up 143
Looking Back to the Effects of Childhood Goodbyes: Getting Real 143
Say What You Feel 144
It's Not Your Fault 144
You Have a Right to Feel Resentful 145
Have No Regrets 146

Teens' Final Conversations: A Crash Course in Adulthood 147
You'll Grow Up Fast 147
Feel Empathy If You Can, but Forgive Yourself If You Can't 148

Young Adults' Final Conversations: Challenges in Changing Times 149
Embrace Your Imperfection 150
Don't Wait; Say It Now 150

Mature Adults: Getting Real (Again) and So Imperfect 151
You Won't Always Be in Control 152
Clean Up the Relationship 152

SUMMARY 154
TIPS FOR BETTER CONVERSATIONS 154

Chapter 13: Going On 157
Lessons Learned: New Ways of Being 157
"More Life!" Joy, Energy, Spirit 157
Slow Down and Take the Time 158
Stop "Walking on Eggshells" 159
Break the Rules! 160
Know Your Feelings, Then Voice Them 162
Release Control: Let It Unfold 162
No Fear, No Regrets 164
New Plans, New Paths 165
Time to Take Charge of My Life 165
Relationships: Cherish Your Intimates and Love Again 165
Education: New Personal Goals 167
Career: New Contributions 168
SUMMARY 169
LOOSENING UP 169
RESETTING LIFE'S DEFAULTS 169
TIPS FOR BETTER CONVERSATIONS 170

Chapter 14: The Conversation Continues Beyond Death 173
Death Does Not End the Relationship 173
Real-Time Messages 174
Sensory Experiences 174
Touch 174
Vision 174
Scent 175
Sound 175
Signs from the Departed 175
Meaningful Objects 176
Signs in the Natural World: Birds, Butterflies, Flowers 177
Nudges to Remind Us: Moving Memories and Flickering Lights 178
Near-Death Contact 180
Dreamtime Messages 182
Dreams with Specific Messages 182
"I Am Sorry I Had to Leave" 182
"I Am Waiting for Her" 182
Dreams That Bring Peace 183
"I Love You Still" 183
"Don't Worry; I Am Fine" 184
SUMMARY 184
TIPS FOR BETTER CONVERSATIONS 185

PART FOUR: YOUR FINAL CONVERSATIONS

Chapter 15: We Never Said It Was Easy 189

Avoiding Final Conversations 189
Obstacles to Final Conversations 190
- Topics Avoided 191
- A Lack of Privacy 192
- Suppressing Emotions 192
  - Family Norms 192
  - Personal Expectations 193
- Pressure of Time 193
- Health Barriers to Communication (Mental and Physical) 195
  - Dementia Impairments 195
  - Unconsciousness and Other Physical Health Obstacles 196
- Drawbacks of Technology 197
- Individual Challenges 198

Approaching Final Conversations 199

SUMMARY 200
TIPS FOR BETTER CONVERSATIONS 201

Chapter 16: You Can Too: Communication Skills for the Last Day and Every Day 203

Why Engage in Final Conversations? 204
How to Prepare for Final Conversations 205
- Your Availability 206
- Timing Your Visit 206
- Choosing the Place 206
- Privacy 207
- Frequency and Duration 207
- The Caregiver's Role 207
- Limitations 208

How to Communicate with Skill 208
- Listening 209
  - Give Yourself a Reason to Listen Carefully 209
  - Be Other-Centered 209
  - Stop Talking 209
  - Get Out of Your Own Head 209
- Speaking 209
  - Ask a Question 209
  - Paraphrase Your Loved One's Statement 210
  - Do Perception Checks 211
  - Say What You Feel 211

Being Silent 212
Pay Attention to Nonverbal Communication 212
Be There 212
When to Ask for Help 212
Medical and Caregiving Professionals 213
Limitations: Interaction When the Dying's Senses Are Impaired 214
Getting Through the Grief 215

SUMMARY 216

About the Authors 218

NOTES ON TERMINOLOGY

We created the following terms for consistency and simplicity throughout the book.

Final Conversations: all verbal and nonverbal communication that occurs between the Living and the Dying, from the diagnosis of a terminal illness to the moment of death.

The Living: the interviewee, the person who spoke to us about the final conversation(s) after the death of their loved one, the one who will continue living.

The Dying: the Living's loved one who was dying.

Spiritual Message: any message beyond the scientifically observable sort. Some of the Living considered them to be related to religion or faith; others considered them to be metaphysical phenomena beyond rational explanation.

> **Note:** Some participants insisted that we use their given first name, while others asked that we use a pseudonym. Some of our participants were anonymous, and they were also given an arbitrary first name. We respected their wishes.

ACKNOWLEDGMENTS

We appreciate all the sources of support that have come our way during the life of this project. Some of these appear below, some we may have forgotten to name—please forgive us if we have missed you—and some have simply arrived without a name and face to thank. But we are grateful for everyone; you lifted and carried us through our journey. We acknowledge:

The Dying for their inspiration.

The Living, our interviewees and survey participants, for their heartfelt contributions. Even if some stories were not a good fit for this book, the project would not have been completed without hearing everyone's story—they all taught us what final conversations are about and how they help to transform lives following the death of loved ones.

Texas State University and Maureen's colleagues in the Department of Communication Studies for their support for her program of research exploring final conversations at the end of life for the past two decades.

California State Polytechnic at Humboldt for their support of data collection and transcription in the earlier phase of the study.

Meredith Rutter, former editor of VanderWyk & Burnham, for publishing our first book and for her advice to join the Authors Guild for help in retaining our rights to the material.

Dan Riordan and Bill Sheehan for their kind and generous advice about social media marketing.

Over 20 years of academic research on final conversations were enhanced by colleagues and academic co-authors who worked with Maureen as she collected, analyzed, interpreted, and wrote academic journal articles and book chapters. A very special thanks to Mark Generous, who helped Maureen with two major final conversations, data collections, quantitative data analysis, and the nine academic articles that he co-authored with her. Another special thanks to Paula Baldwin, who helped Maureen conduct interviews with children and adolescents about their final conversations, as well as two articles that she co-authored with her. Additionally, thanks to co-authors Dana Hansen, Jody Koenig Kellas, Lauren Lee, and Valerie Manusov, with whom Maureen published one article each on final conversations.

Those who read parts or all of our manuscript for us and gave us encouraging and helpful feedback: Deborah Brady, Susan Bruner, Carissa Duval, Mark Generous, Mark Vassberg, Rick Davids, and Verlinda Thompson. Thank you, Carissa Hoopes, for gorgeous photos from a gorgeous photographer.

Julie's husband, Rick Davids, supported this project by his creation of e-mail lists, his walks with the dog, their mutual laughter, and his love. Maureen's husband, Mark Vassberg, along with their children, Ian and Meagan, were cheerleaders and a constant source of love and day-to-day support.

Our parents: Eileen and Howard Yingling, Thomas and Patricia Keeley, and Maureen's in-laws, David and Liliane Vassberg, for starting us talking and for continuing the conversation. Julie's siblings: Pat, Ray, Terry, and Mike, for floating through life and death with Julie; and Maureen's siblings: Colleen, Kit, Chris, Jim, and Kevin, for accompanying one another through the final conversations that continued throughout our parents' and other family members' deaths.

Friends who gave us emotional support and encouragement: Carissa, Valerie, Susan, Verlinda, Amanda, Mark, Melinda, Jody, Deborah, Linda, Lynn, and Sue.

Finally, we'd like to thank our editor, Sally Mason-Swaab, and the entire team at Hay House.

We have been honored and privileged to have been the recipients of these stories and to have been able to share a complete picture of what final conversations look like, our understanding about the challenges and benefits of participating in final conversations, as well as the transformative nature of final conversations at the end of life.

part one

UNDERSTANDING FINAL CONVERSATIONS

chapter 1

Finding the Good in Goodbye

I am so grateful for the wisdom my grandmother shared with me. Our final conversation serves as my mantra. My life and my daughter's life are a direct reflection of the wisdom she shared. It's almost as if she gave me a guidebook. She was brutally honest with me regarding my flaws and the tendencies I possessed that would be my barriers in life. I am so grateful for our final conversation. The memory of our final conversation is still so fresh, and its recording plays whenever I have to make a major decision. (Olivia)

When death comes for the one you love, you have the chance to say what needs to be said and to be enriched by the good goodbye. What is a good goodbye? It is a last chance to say, "I love you," an experience that leaves us with no regrets, and an opportunity to create new memories of a loved one that can leave us changed forever and for the better. We so firmly believe that you can be transformed by the good goodbye that we wrote this book to share what hundreds of people have told us about their final conversations. We know that most of you already have the necessary skills to do so. But many of you have never witnessed final conversations because they so often occur behind closed doors. That apparent secrecy can create uncertainty and fear. In this book, we share examples from hundreds of people who have already experienced final conversations, and along the way, we give suggestions to help you have a good goodbye.

FINAL CONVERSATIONS THAT TRANSFORM US

What Are Final Conversations?

All the communicative acts between loved ones, beginning with the sure knowledge that one of them is dying and ending with the moment of death. They include all those moments of talking, touching, and spending time with the Dying at the end of life, when moments are cherished and awareness of the value of their time together is heightened.

Transformation

To transform is to shift how we see the world, how we understand what's happening in our lives, how we adapt to the trials we endure. So how can final conversations at the end of life lead to transformation? We share transformation stories from each of six themes. The first theme, and the most universal, is love. These are messages that strengthen our emotional connection with our dying loved ones. The second theme is everyday talk or the sorts of mundane messages and activities that continue the relationship to the very end and make new memories in the process. The third, taking care of business, often concerns the Dying's final wishes for the Living to take care of what they need now and after they are gone. The fourth theme, the Living's identity, appears in messages that speak to the Living's strengths, talents, and sometimes weaknesses. They encourage us to accept the best part of ourselves and pursue the life we want. The fifth theme, spiritual experiences, allows us to witness the proximity of the Dying to their afterlife. Finally, for those in difficult and damaged relationships, the sixth theme is about finding a way to heal and forgive before it is too late.

THE SURPRISING GIFTS THAT COME FROM FINAL CONVERSATIONS

We hear from those who have participated in final conversations that there are gifts bestowed by a good goodbye.

Gifts for the Dying

The Dying most often prefer to spend their final days in peace. And they will let us know whom they want to speak with before they go. Often, death is accepted only after the desired loved ones have made it to the deathbed for that final word or touch. They want to tell their intimates to move on, to live well, and to carry their love always. In these ways, the Dying find closure, peace, and a willingness to release life.

Gifts for the Living

Final conversations helped many find closure with the Dying loved one. More importantly, many reported having no regrets as their loved one approached death. And having no regrets meant that there was no need for guilt and every reason to grieve well. Grief is inevitable with deep loss. But those who are there at the end, knowing they will continue to cherish the relationship, are those who will not be crushed by grief but instead accept its bittersweet ebb and flow. Individuals who have open, honest, and authentic conversations with the Dying are more equipped to cope with their loss. They recognize the diminished quality of life for the Dying loved one and come to see that death is a natural part of life. They realize that it is okay to feel whatever emotions come up at the end of life and that ultimately death brings release for their loved one.

Then there is the personal growth that begins as a seed planted by the Dying while the Living walks the path to death with them. That seed can grow into a mature tree of self-knowledge over the months and years nourished by remembrance and reflection. A child facing the death of a loved one often emotionally matures beyond their years, particularly when the Dying one communicates truthfully and openly with them. Adults often find new ways of thinking, new ways of relating, a renewed passion for life, or a new path to pursue. For some, these changes are immediate. For others, recognizing the shift in self may take weeks, months, or even years following the death of the loved one.

If these gifts are available by participating with the Dying in last interactions, why do so many people avoid them? Because we live in a culture that fosters fear of all things associated with death and dying. Most people try to steer clear of the topic as much as possible. We will all face the death of a loved one. And many will feel unprepared. It may help to understand the fears.

FEAR OF DEATH AND DYING

Death is one thing we cannot control. No matter what the medical industry may lead you to believe about it, death is not a disease. It is a natural process. We will all face the death of a loved one. And often we will feel unprepared. When Julie called her sister Pat to tell her that their mother had died, Pat said "I wasn't ready." Julie replied, "She was." Death will not wait until you are ready to come for those you love. So, let's address what makes us shrink from it.

Fear of the Unknown

Generations ago, death occurred naturally at home. The loved one had the chance to say goodbye in a comfortable and quiet setting. The body was washed and dressed by beloved kin, and then laid out in the parlor so that neighbors and friends could see the last of the departed and commiserate with the grieving. But no more. Death has been claimed by a medical industry bent on keeping patients alive for as long as possible. And that means that when all medical interventions fail, death occurs amid beeping machines, invasive tubes, and a cluster of strangers. And their loved ones are left out of the equation, not knowing what a natural death looks like.

Most of us wish to die at home. But often we end up dying in hospitals and nursing homes. Medical staff may prefer a quick, clean death, but it runs counter to what we consider a good death. A good death includes time to have intimate words with loved ones.

Fear of the Pain of Loss

Grief is inevitable after a loss. It can be avoided no more than death can. You will feel pain with the absence of a loved one. That pain will ebb and flow, recede and come roaring back, though the cycles become less intense with time. But a good goodbye can allay the pain of grief in the knowledge that we said what we needed to say, that we heard what the Dying wanted to tell us, that we did our best to make their final moments loving ones. The truth is that when we accept that death is approaching, it creates a newfound opportunity to capture the gifts of *terminal time*: a time when we prioritize our relationship with the Dying, when we can slow down the world and say no to all the everyday trivia that usually takes up our time and focus on what is truly important. So, we invite you to participate in final conversations. Let us show you what they look like and share with you our recommendations on the best way to do them.

WHAT WILL YOU FIND HERE?

Real Stories from Real People

Hundreds of people have told us their stories. Some conversations were hard to start; some felt easy and flowed freely. But no one regretted having them, though some regretted not having more of them. The simplest advice we heard from them was to put aside the time and just be there with your loved one as often as you can. The most complex responses included that it wasn't easy, but it was necessary; it was worth the time and effort; and it was a skill that can be practiced.

Advice from Communication Experts

As the authors of this book, our combined experience totals 65 years of teaching, research, and writing about communication. We both had experienced the death of loved ones and had gone looking for the best ways to communicate with them at the end of life. We were disappointed to find so little about communication between the Dying and their loved ones. We wanted to fill that gap. We agreed to work together to find more about communication practices near death and have been doing so for the past 20 years. We want to share what we have found out with everyone who is facing the death of a loved one with no clue of how to go about it.

HOW TO USE THIS BOOK

Find What You Need

Some of you will want to read the book from start to finish, while others may want to browse around to find what they may need right now. We include details in the Table of Contents so that you can find what you're looking for as needed. Poke around, read a few stories, check the last pages of each chapter for a Summary section and Tips for Better Conversations that may give you direction. If you need more direction and are ready to have the conversations, go to the last chapters in the section, Your Final Conversations, for hints about successful communication and getting started.

Enjoy the Stories

Find the stories that speak to you by theme. Explore the ways people have changed from saying the good goodbye under the Outcomes section. These will give you a good idea of what to expect and possible gifts you will receive. Of course, every final conversation is unique to the relationship, but you will find some comfort from knowing others have gone before you and have had similar experiences. The core message that we hope that you take away from this book:

Be there. Listen. Love.

Be grateful for the opportunity to have a good goodbye.

chapter 2

What's Culture Got to Do with It?

Honestly, I feel your culture shapes who you are whether you like it or not. We view death as something that happens to everyone and is unavoidable. In many ways it's used to inspire people to live their lives to the fullest. (Arya)

Arya expresses two beliefs about death and dying that she attributes to her culture: First, that death is inevitable and unavoidable. Second, that this inescapability of death inspires us to live life to the fullest. These beliefs are not universally held and demonstrate an openness, acceptance, and a positive view of death and dying that is not shared by all people or cultures.

We know death well enough. Or so we think. We stream movies that show us faked deaths that are either violent and gory or calm and silent. We go to wakes and funerals where we witness the sorrow of those left behind and a serene, perfectly made-up face in the casket. But not the hard realities that led there. Those who are prepared for those realities may claim a cultural background that still includes death as a part of living. When did death disappear from us, except at a distance, through a screen? When our cultural beliefs about death and dying shifted.

CULTURAL BELIEFS ABOUT DEATH AND DYING

We understand culture as the set of customary beliefs, social behaviors, and habits of an ethnic, religious, familial, or generational group that are based on our interactions with family members, friends, church, ethnic affiliations, and more. Many of the comments to follow treat ***family*** as a culture. Some comment on the conflicting messages they get between family and the larger culture. Some feel that their traditions and beliefs are changing from one ***generation*** to the next, so in some ways, a generational grouping can be a culture as well. Julie recalls her mother's reaction when we began to study end-of-life communication: *"I don't understand why you would have these conversations."* She was not alone. Many of her generation (born in the 1920s, coming of age in World War II) were different sorts of communicators, not given to discussing relationships or emotions.

Americans are a mixed bag. We all, except Indigenous Americans, come from somewhere else, whether that was 10 years ago or 400 years ago. Some ethnic groupings keep their cultural traditions alive, and some assimilate. Considering the forces of assimilation at work over the course of generations, we think that there are some broad beliefs and practices about final conversations for most Americans. Through our research we found a range of beliefs on three topics: the role of death in life, communication about death, and social interaction with the Dying.

The Role of Death in Life: Avoidance or Acceptance

We know that some people feel ambivalent about death and dying, or even find themselves having to straddle seeming contradictions between two cultures. Although there was a broad range of beliefs expressed, most fell on a continuum from a completely negative view of the topic to a more positive approach to death and dying. Somewhere between the two extremes, we find acceptance of the inevitability of death and the capacity to cope with its effects.

Death Is the Enemy: We Avoid It

What we do not know, we often fear. And fear of death leads to avoiding the topic of death. In the larger American culture, death has been removed from our homes and our view to medical settings. Harriet specifies how we came to silence death: *My culture attempts to hide or deny death in general; we are very uncomfortable with the entire idea. Today, most people die in hospitals (despite the wishes of most) and are buried by funeral homes. Service industries have emerged to allow us to get away from the unpleasant issues. I am concerned that unhealthy attitudes about death make some people prolong their lives for too long or make medical choices that are futile rather than face death.*

More and more often, people tell us that their intuitive responses do not match the cultural norms based on fear and negativity. Indeed, some point to the contrast between the norms they've learned and the beliefs they are consciously pursuing. Rhonda told us: *My dad has no inner monologue and is intent on talking about depressing things. Because of him I try to think of only positive things. When someone dies, he will talk continuously about how the person died and the odds of someone else dying of that affliction. I talk instead of happier memories of the deceased. When my uncle Frank died of diabetes, I didn't feel sadness at his funeral. Instead, I had to stop myself from laughing at past memories so I wouldn't disturb other mourners.*

Death Is a Natural Part of Life: We Accept It

Some ethnic groups stray from the current norm based on their ease with the inevitability of death. When death is a natural part of life, it may be seen as another milestone like birth, puberty, and old age, leading to acceptance and a more positive and celebrated approach to death. The influence of a culture that celebrates all its turning points may ease a death belief into approach rather than avoidance. As Kisha put it: *Death is inevitable; it is how you cope with loved ones dying that is the challenge.* Everyone can admit that death is inevitable, but when it comes down to that "lived experience" there are a variety of responses, from performing traditional rituals to more individualized conscious actions, that allow the Living to accompany the Dying through this natural stage of life.

Family Norms. A few who spoke with us grew up in families that escaped American cultural norms. They kept their loved ones at home where they could maintain the relationship for as long as possible. Carlos told us: *I grew up in a culture where we took care of our sick at home. We were all around the dying person and engaged in conversations all the time.* Sofia's family also accepted death by making the most of their remaining time together. *My family made me view death as something that helps people come together. They made it known that death happens to everybody and the only way to help get through it is by making the best of the time you have left with them.*

Cultural Effects. Because religion and life philosophies are so entwined with culture, we found quite a few examples of a death-as-natural belief system among Hispanic family members. Roberta shared: *I've always been taught that death is inevitable. Being Hispanic, we have quite a lot of people in our family, which can be quite the party, but then again it can be quite the funeral as well. Because we have a big family, we have a lot of deaths in the family as well. Everyone has to die. It is a sad thing to experience, but it's just how life works.* This response feels like an acceptance of death that is cushioned by the support of a large family. In the context of close-knit families, death becomes another important event to experience together.

Buddhists do not necessarily believe in a god but believe in the importance of compassion in this life to ensure a happy afterlife. As Tae sees it, *When people die, they are sent to heaven. Even if you don't believe in god, Buddhism is a way of life, and that is just the way it is in our family. Death is a part of life, and to be a good person was a thing everyone in our family stressed about.* This example verges on a positive approach to death for those who have lived the Buddhist way and feel confident of their afterlife.

Mixed Messages. The kind of memorializing traditional in Mexico would be out of place in the U.S. *In my culture, death is such a big thing to happen, you mourn for months and even years. Having moved to the U.S. from Mexico made it different for me because here it is obviously a bad thing that happens, but I feel like you make a big deal out of it for a week or even less and move on.* The sort of traditions that make losing a loved one bearable and even celebratory become eroded in a culture that does not value them. As a result of this mix of different cultures, some of us must learn to make sense of conflicting messages about death.

American culture does not prepare us for dealing with death except by avoiding it. Some families may soften that message by saying death is inevitable, but in the same breath, conveying distinct disapproval of emotional expression of grief. Loss and grief are inevitable and cannot be denied forever. But people try by giving death the silent treatment.

COMMUNICATION ABOUT DEATH: SILENCE OR OPENNESS

Silence and Secrets

The most common comments we heard about cultural beliefs were those that referenced a ban on talk about death and dying. *It is just not talked about; it is like it is avoided; it is a taboo topic.* That's the short answer from Mary Jane and pretty accurate. Elaine fought this taboo and overcame her fear of death. *I was not distant. I was right there, holding her hand until the very end. Our culture doesn't have a mechanism to discuss that level of lived experience with death. We have no training in death. We put on a happy face and try to move things to a lighter topic. We don't know how to revere the experience of witnessing death.* Clearly, we have lost the art of the "lived experience" of death. The medicalization of death has made it challenging to hold the Dying one's hand to the end, never mind having the freedom to authentically interact with them. The taboo against talking about death and dying is a surefire avoidance technique. If we don't talk about it, we don't have to think about it, and we certainly don't have to feel about it. For now.

Family Norms. Most of us simply didn't hear or speak of death to anyone when young, so talk of death is never practiced enough to become comfortable and feel normal with. Mary Beth confirms: *Death wasn't around much growing up. I never had a family member or anyone close to me die until I was 13 and then again when I was 15, so even by the second death the communication was fairly light. We didn't speak much about the actual action of death but mainly of the person or the events surrounding it. We didn't know how to talk about it.*

Cultural Effects. Considering the comfort with which some Hispanic people reported viewing death, talking about it at the end of life was another matter. Berto shared, *We were a close cultural family, but we didn't share many intimate conversations. In Mexico culture we* *were close but respectful; therefore, we must keep conversations and shows of affection respectful.*

Mariana addressed not only the silence but pointed out the problems. She told us that many Hispanics die without considering the plans for their estates. *Latino culture does not talk about what is going to happen at the time of death or afterwards. That is the reason not many Latinos have a will.*

In China, death and dying are not discussed, and particularly not with the Dying one. They care for the Dying but are not straightforward about the fact that death is imminent. Mei told us that *people in China always conceal the illness the Dying has and tell the Dying that they are fine. In that way, we think those Dying can live longer than those who know what illness they have, especially for cancer. Sometimes Dying might not know they have cancer until the last minutes of life, or they never know, but they have the feeling that they have some serious illnesses. People around Dying just pretend to be happy and give almost everything to the Dying; they try their best to help the Dying to make their wishes come true, from the favorite food to the place the Dying wanted to go. I have the feeling that I view death and dying quite differently from those who come from other cultures.* Mei is a U.S. resident still steeped in Chinese culture but who suspects that we in the United States do not do this. We suspect some *do* keep information from the Dying, perhaps for their own comfort or when they deem the Dying to be unable to use the information—perhaps because of the onset of dementia or some other condition that affects decision-making and planning.

Mixed Messages. Confusion can ensue when cultural traditions blend or contrast. Ray explains: *Nationality-wise I am half Chinese and Polish/Italian. Prior to my stepfather's death, death hadn't been discussed at all in my household; I hadn't had anyone in my life pass away. Once my stepfather died, we did not really discuss what had happened. He was there one day and not the next. I had to kind of figure things out on my own, which was difficult at the age of 10. It wasn't until I was in high school/college that I fully understood what happened and was able to navigate my memories and thoughts I had had during that time.* A child left with silence during and after his parent's death may be very confused for a long time and may need help sorting out the reality and importance of the death. When the parents' cultures collide, the child may need an adult who can speak with them about the reality of death, and how disparate traditions and beliefs can be adapted when they intersect or even clash.

Many of those faced with mixed messages do adapt and change. Quite a few of the Living spoke about how they changed their approach to death and dying from the one they learned from family and culture to one they found personally more useful. Some of these shifts were spurred by their work culture, and some learned from the experience of being fully present with a loved one through their death.

Charlotte learned how to paste a happy face on death and dying from her family. However, when her friend moved in and both knew he was dying, she learned to talk daily with her friend, in contrast to the silence around them. *I feel like people in my culture mourn the death while having a positive outlook—"they are in a better place" kind of ideology. In my family, we mostly try to just push out the idea of the death of loved ones, as with any other difficult situation. The people around me mostly didn't talk about the inevitability of my friend's death. Me and my friend mostly had final conversations while alone and wouldn't mention these rituals to others. We took that into our own hands. We would talk every day he was living with us up until the day he passed.*

Lynnette points to a generational difference between parents who don't want to talk about anything related to death, including wills and advanced directives, and a child who wants to know what their wishes are. *In my immediate family, my mom still has not composed her will, and I feel odd being the one to bring it up. I am sure my dad has, but I asked him once and he looked at me funny and said it was "morbid" to ask. It's almost like my mom thinks it is tempting fate to write her will, when I feel like it is the opposite. . . . I personally wouldn't have a problem discussing things like what measures I would want to be taken—how long I'd like to be kept alive by machines and things like that. My parents, however, are very uncomfortable with me saying things like that, especially about myself.* What we see here is a clash of cultures; in this case the cultures are generational. In the next case, the difference has more to do with spatial distance than the passage of time.

We have become a mobile culture in which professionals are expected to move their families if they wish to advance in their careers. The result is that the extended family is often spread across the country and no longer is a close-knit unit and source of support in difficult times. For Brian, *If the death is from an extended part of the family, it doesn't hurt as much unless we were particularly close. If that family member lives in a different state and we haven't conversed or seen each other in years, it's almost like a stranger died or is dying.* When a relative has not been a part of your recent life, it may not only be hard to know how to talk about the death prior to the end, but it may also be difficult to make plans to honor the death or support living kin. Therefore, silence can be the only response that doesn't feel weird and forced.

Open, Honest Talks

Family Norms. Few Americans grow up with open communication about death and dying. Those who did said that although they were sad for their own loss, they were at peace with the goodbyes they expressed. Ron put it this way: *I view death/dying with sadness for myself and the other people who feel the loss but also with a relief that the Dying is no longer suffering. My parents taught me to make sure that I always told the Dying that I loved them and to help them whenever and however I could leading up to when they passed.* Kit mentioned that communication with the Dying is a positive way for the Living to deal with the stress of death. *My parents taught me to make the Dying comfortable and express how much they mean to you. Telling them how much you appreciate and love them is the best way to cope with somebody close to you dying.*

Cultural Effects. Many who reported talk about death did not necessarily talk about it with the one who was dying. James, from a small town in Texas, said: *Death is something that is pretty open in the culture around me. People realize that in order to get over the death of your loved one and healthily move on, you have to talk about it sometimes. Death is viewed as just part of life, and it's something everyone must go through.*

Both German and Dutch heritage bring a practical streak of dealing with what must be done. The Dying, by being down-to-earth about their dying process, may open the lines of communication. Heidi shared: *I came from a German family, and my mother was very pragmatic in her views. She was matter of fact about dying.* Having a German mother who was very practical led this woman to do a lot of soul searching leading up to her mother's death. Heidi continued, *My mother had long said she was not afraid to die, so fear wasn't part of her experience. By my mother's final week, that process was over and I was happy with where the journey had taken me, and I definitely did feel stronger as a result.*

Mixed Messages. For Henri, all the talking occurs after the death and not before. *Culture has made it easier for me to discuss death and dying because I can talk about it in a positive way. I can discuss our memories and our final conversations without getting too emotional because our culture taught me to be strong after a death.* Of course, it's much easier to discuss death and the Dying once they are gone and we are a bit distanced from our emotions. As James discovered, it's easier to talk with other people and not with the Dying. *My brother and sister and I talked about the situation matter-of-factly. Sometimes, though, my sister and I would have very emotional conversations outside of my brother's hospice room because we didn't want to face him directly.* Although this expression of emotions to others may save the Dying some distress, it also may fail to give them the opportunity to say what they would like to say or hear what they would like to hear.

Overall, we received very few examples from people who believe that we should talk with the dying loved one directly about their experience. And perhaps that is why so many fail to show up at the end of a loved one's life.

COMPANY AT THE END: ALONE OR TOGETHER

Dying in Isolation

"I want to die alone" said no one, ever. We all hope to be in the loving arms of family when we go. Of course, the Dying may choose to take their last breath alone perhaps to spare the Living, but the desire to have loved ones hold you before the end is universal. Sadly, because so many deaths occur in hospitals, hooked up to machinery and isolated at least part of the time, many do die alone. And sometimes, the Living at a distance simply cannot get there in time.

Greater emphasis in recent generations on careers and the subsequent expectation of mobility has led many Americans to feel guilt when they are not available for their families and loved ones. Harold shared: *The spread of my relatives throughout the world to tend to their careers crippled my connection with those that I could have known even better before they passed away. Coming from a hardworking, middle class, Caucasian family inhibits our relatives from being within as close proximity to each other as we all would like, especially in times of tragedy. Careers come before family sometimes, and that is frustrating when the time at work could have been better spent with those that would so unexpectedly perish.*

The generation gap between Connie and her parents in the following example was clearly related to career, and the guilt that ensued is palpable. *Our culture, mine included, doesn't revere the elderly and care for them. In other cultures, it is an honor; in ours it is a bother, though we don't want to face that. We are so committed to our obligations that we can't care for our families. Part of the problem is nuclear families, separated and unable to all pitch in when needed. So, I felt helpless when it came to being able to care for my folks when they needed me. I couldn't work and be a 24/7 caretaker. So, all this influences how I feel about their dying experience. In retrospect, I wish I had done more, but have come to terms with the fact that I did about as well as I could during the circumstances.* The mobility so widespread in the U.S. has a chilling effect on the kind of company the Dying may wish for and expect. The much-vaunted claim that the loved one was "surrounded by family" may not be as common as the obituary columns report.

Dying in Close Relationship

For most people, except those separated either emotionally or physically, family is your support when death approaches. Xander shared: *I experienced death and dying at a young age and often. I was taught that it is something that happens, and with our family and faith, we can make it through anything. We are open about it in our family and talk with our loved ones often and share our memories of them after they are gone.*

Most from a Hispanic culture, like Mateo, talked about the importance of extended family. *Being from a border town, sharing time together was essential due to traveling back and forth between cities, which is common for families along the El Paso–Juarez area. During the dying process, we gather to talk, pray, and support one another. After the loved one has passed, we seek comfort in our families, not just immediate, but extended as well.*

The experience of death is an exclusive one for some cultures. It is for family alone and specifically does not include outsiders. Santiago confirms: *Often, we speak among our own families and will not express ourselves with other people. We keep our feelings to ourselves.*

SUMMARY

The stories in this chapter came from people from all over the country. Recent immigrants gave the impression either of comfort in long-held traditions or of discomfort and confusion that may arise from trying to assimilate American practices to more traditional ones. Although traditions vary greatly, we can simplify somewhat by taking a broad view of three clusters of beliefs: Traditional, Standard American, and Emergent.

Traditional

In general, members of older, more traditional cultures (Hispanic, African, Korean, for example) tend to believe that death is a natural part of life, that it is a family experience, that the Dying is to be celebrated, and talk of death is allowed, although within set limits.

Standard American

On the other hand, American culture, having surrendered death to the medical industry, evolved a set of beliefs to deal with that disconnect: that death is the enemy, that it is often an individual experience, that the Living should move on, and that it's best not to talk about it.

In the Traditional system, the tendency is to accept death as inevitable. In the standard American system, the inclination is to avoid both talk of death and participation in the dying process. It isn't Americans' fault, but is a side effect of rapid advances in medical science and an overemphasis on keeping people alive simply because we can, despite the tradeoffs made for quality of life.

Emergent

However, there is a third way. Quite a few respondents felt torn between two cultures (family/ethnicity versus larger culture), two ethnicities, or two generations. These are the people who are paving a new way for Americans to experience death. To relieve the discomfort of dissonant beliefs, they are rejecting either the American beliefs or the beliefs of an older culture that no longer serve them. They question the tendency to avoid death. They accept death as a "lived experience"; they try to be the involved family even to friends as they are dying. They approach both celebration and mourning as equally valuable. And they positively approach talk about death with the Dying and with others. They are at the cutting edge of change in American beliefs and behaviors around death.

TIPS FOR BETTER CONVERSATIONS

Perspectives on death and dying from across the globe vary a great deal. There are as many ways to approach (or avoid) death as there are human groupings. When others cope with death and dying in a different fashion than you do, remember there is no "right" way, but many ways. Be conscious of what you have absorbed from your culture and how you choose to create your own beliefs and traditions.

- Death is inevitable, but resignation is not the only response to it. There are gifts to be had from conversing with the Dying; they are to be found in the stories that follow in this book. Allow yourself to feel some interest, some positive approach, to walking the final road with a loved one.
- If you are one of those between two cultures/ethnicities/generations, be patient with yourself and respectful of others' beliefs. If your child is the one caught in the culture clash, talk with them about what they think is good or challenging about each way of thinking.

- No matter how you handle it, know you are not alone, and you are not wrong. Others have been where you are. And if you wish to challenge cultural norms, take it a step at a time. Many in the U.S., including hospice workers and other caregivers, see that the norms of the previous generation are not serving us. The medicalization of death changed everything, but you can take back the dying experience so it is the uplifting and satisfying experience you may wish to own.

chapter 3

Beyond Words: Nonverbal Messages

The last "conversation" I had was all nonverbal. She turned her head to me, and I caressed her cheek with my hand, kissed her, and then just stayed with her until the end. It was sad, but very peaceful. I am thankful to have been there and to let her know I loved her. Those 36 hours will always be with me. (Hailey)

Although words create much of the intellectual meaning of final conversations, these last interactions are often less about a meeting of the minds and more about emotional and relational connection. These unspoken messages give the Living and the Dying a way to share, without words, messages of love, comfort, and closure.

Furthermore, during the last days and final hours of life, the Dying often deals with a wide variety of symptoms such as shortness of breath, dry mouth, or overwhelming sleepiness. Their bodies are often shutting down, making them physically incapable of verbal communication, thereby leaving them totally dependent upon nonverbal channels of communication. Nonverbal communication can bring information and consolation to the Living because the Dying can communicate with them even when words are no longer physically possible.

Nonverbal communication is every unspoken act between two people that carries meaning for them. We have at least eight ways to communicate in relationships without the use of words:

- ***Body language:*** the eyes, face, and body communicate in combination to express feelings such as love, anger, or frustration.
- *Voices* can hum, cry, sigh, and so on to modify words or to convey specialized meaning for partners. Even silence may be significant.
- *Touch* such as kisses, hugs, gentle pressure, or holding hands can signal love, affection, and recognition.
- ***Proximity:*** being in the Dying's space or sitting next to them sends a message of caring and essentially creates the opportunity for final conversations.
- *Time* set aside to be with and care for the Dying conveys a willingness to rearrange life to be with the Dying as top priority.
- ***Tokens of love*** (e.g., flowers, gifts) and ***material possessions*** (e.g., photos, jewelry, stuffed animals) can trigger memories from final conversations, help create a soothing environment for both the Living and the Dying at the end of life, and serve as reminders of the loved one in the Living's future.
- ***Smells*** such as using aromatherapy to soothe and provide comfort, or removing smells that are too strong and cause discomfort to the Dying.
- ***Physical appearance*** of the Dying as they go through the dying process can be disturbing but is also very revealing of the state of the human body at the end of life.

SEE ME; FEEL ME; HEAR ME; TOUCH ME

Eyes: Windows to the Soul

The Living often talked about the gift of a final connection in the form of eye contact at the last moment of life. Victoria shared specifics with us about the power and meaning of a final look between her and her husband, Kerry. *I just walked over and took his hand, and he opened his eyes and looked at me and died. And there was a real sense of peace . . . at the very end just having him look at me one last time. There was tremendous love and tenderness in that look.*

Maureen's mother came back from between worlds to say a private goodbye to Maureen's father, Tom. She recalls the story: *Pat had been in a coma for a day and a half, Tom had been holding her hand, kissing her cheek, and sitting by her side for two hours when suddenly Pat came out of her coma and looked at him. Tom stood up, kissed her, and said, "Pat, I love you," then she took one last breath and died. A window had opened momentarily, and she had come out of her coma to share one last look to say goodbye to her beloved husband.* Pat's private goodbye through a last shared glance between the two of them was a powerful message of love for Tom that remained with him until his own death. A final look exchanged between the Living and the Dying is not uncommon, and it is remembered and cherished by those who are fortunate to know that final connection.

Eye contact can also tell the Living that they matter, that they are significant to the Dying. For example, Ruth, who was young when her father died, talks about the eye contact that he made with her during one of their interactions. *He made eye contact with me and that was important 'cause he was talking to me like I was a real person, not like I was his little four-year-old. My daddy was telling me that "you're going to be alright."* She went on to explain that the fact that he had made direct eye contact with her made all the difference in the world to her becoming a successful and mature adult.

Face Reveals Emotion; Body Conveys the Intensity of the Emotion

Facial expressions reveal people's emotions, for example, a frown. The intensity of the emotion is often revealed in the body and increases awareness about how strongly they are feeling. For example, if the frowner is also clenching their hands and tensing their neck, then we assume they are quite angry. All three cues together help us know how to react.

A positive nonverbal expression can be a breath of fresh air that releases stress in a trying situation. For instance, the unexpected smile from Maureen's mom, Pat, who at her end of life, normally only saw grays and shadows, *smiled when she saw her year-old grandson's blue eyes, because the light from the window behind her hit them just right as he balanced himself on the coffee table in front of her.* Or the laughter shared by Ted's family as they sat together *sharing stories and laughing on the last night that they gathered before their father died.*

Negative nonverbal expressions can be upsetting, but they also reveal important information in close relationships. Emily was with her best friend Jeanette when something happened that scared them both during their end-of-life journey: *I was holding her hand when an IV line ran out and spilled onto her hand, and she looked up at me, and I could see the fear in her face and heard it in her voice. I ran and got help. They got in there quickly, and I saw the relief on her face. She didn't say anything, but we both really cried, like sobbed. I mean, like neither of us ever had in each other's presence before, and I think the crying helped both of us. It was very comforting to be able to do that in front of each other. We always laughed heartily together, and here we cried heartily together too. I mean, our souls truly met that day. I know that it was very emotional. I think it was good for both of us. Laughter and tears are good, they are healing, and they are loving.*

Sometimes, however, people are afraid to cry with the Dying or with other family members because they don't want to cause more grief to their loved one; they hope to spare them more sadness and stress. Yet crying together can heal and can bring people even closer. Crying makes both the Living and the Dying more vulnerable and more authentic. SunYin described one such moment: *I had never seen my grandfather cry or even be remotely sad. The day he burst into tears when he saw me crying was probably the most significant bonding moment I had ever had with him.* Being this vulnerable with someone requires trust.

In the same way that tears may fall from joy or fear, anger displays may also signal either ill will or underlying fear. Katherine's mother showed anger to her often through *disapproving looks and once by throwing her dinner plate at the door.* Katherine shared: *While these were not pleasant experiences, I realized that my mother was afraid of dying and that this was the only way that she could communicate it to me.*

Voice: Sounds from the Heart

Waltraud's father was dying in Germany, and she was living in America, so she made frequent phone calls home to her parents. She expected her mother to answer the phone, but once, her dying, silenced father surprised her. *I made one of my regular phone calls to my parents. Mother would answer the phone or nobody. Daddy just let it ring since he couldn't talk anyway. This time, however, after a while, somebody picked up the phone. It wasn't without effort, and I sensed that it must be Daddy since I heard a murmur. "Are you there, Daddy?" "Mama isn't at home?" "I love you!" And then I thought I heard him humming. But I wasn't quite sure, so I listened carefully. "Daddy, are you humming?" I pressed my ear to the receiver, and sure enough, I recognized the melody of the song Daddy was trying to "sing" for me—"Ach, ich hab' in meinem Herzen da drinnen," a song we had sung many times together. It is a loving, melancholic song from the fairy-tale opera* Schwarzer Peter *(Black Peter) by N. Schultze. The first stanza roughly translates into: "Oh, deep in my heart, I feel an awesome pain. All of my flowers I want you to have. And I shall think about you beyond my grave. Oh, deep in my heart, I feel an awesome pain." While Daddy was humming, I was singing quietly along. "Daddy, thank you for singing this song for me, I love you." I knew what he was saying. Four days later he was dead. Daddy didn't die with his song still unsung. And I am still listening to it. I am forever grateful.* A simple tune, carried on by a familiar voice, that has a uniquely shared meaning for both the Living and the Dying can convey love through reminiscence.

Touch: Ways to Connect and to Let Go

Meaningful touch is personal, intimate, and is primarily shared only in close relationships. Touch is powerful in relationships because of the meaning and interpretation that people attribute to it. Touch communicates love, affection, and connection. It discloses unspoken emotions and acknowledgment or understanding. It reveals the type and closeness of a relationship. Touch also gives comfort and consolation. The Living shared with us the types of touch they shared with the Dying and what it meant to them.

Many times, there are multiple forms of touch occurring simultaneously. Selena shared: *I stayed with her day and night until she passed. We both gave each other everything we had to give in life. I held her hand, stroked her cheek, kissed her forehead, and loved her into the next realm.* Sometimes, the last and only way to connect with the Dying is through touch, which may come unexpectedly and on impulse for some relationships. Adam began by describing his relationship: *We were always fully present, but as brothers our lives were characterized by as much anger and hostility as laughter. In the final days my brother was not very coherent or communicative. Close to the end when he was bedridden and barely communicative, I spontaneously kissed him on the forehead. I strongly sensed then and still believe now that we both knew that was "I love you" and "goodbye." No words though. He just very weakly told me, "That was a gift." I knew we were good with each other and that there would be no regrets with how we left each other. He died soon after that. He was right; what a gift this had been for both of us.*

Others spoke to the role of touch for confirming that their dying loved one was still understanding and responding to them. Holland began speaking to his mother, knowing that she could not respond verbally. He explained, *The squeezes from her hand were reiterating that she was understanding even if she couldn't explain or verbally express what she was feeling. While it could've just been muscle spasms at just coincidental spots in our conversation, I felt, I know without a doubt that she understood what I was expressing to her.* Thus, where the two could never quite connect through words during their talks, Holland finally found a way to bond with his dying mother through touch.

Touch can also alleviate suffering and enable people to let each other go. Victoria shared her story about holding her husband, Kerry, as he lay dying. Kerry said to her, *"I want the luxury of being held to earth only by your love. Not to be connected to anything else." That afternoon, I just cuddled up in the bed with him, and he was crying, and then later I went in and we didn't talk because we both felt like words would hold him. And there wasn't any reason to hold him to earth any longer.* Kerry would die later that night, but their afternoon of holding each other helped them to share their love and to ease his pain.

BJ talked about sitting quietly with her dying mother-in-law, Sylvia, and her husband, Stan, with all three of them holding hands until Sylvia felt peaceful enough to let go and to end her fight against her worn-out kidneys. *I decided I was just going to sit with her and hold her. So, I sat down beside her and held her hand. After about 15 or 20 minutes, Stan did the same thing. Within 15 minutes she was dead. I mean, it was so amazing. It just felt so right to be with her that way and to hold her. I finally understood what it meant when someone passes, because I felt her body relax from her head down to her feet, because we were holding her.* The touch shared by BJ, Stan, and Sylvia is more meaningful considering that when Sylvia was healthy, she was not a touchy-feely person. She was someone who would have avoided most attempts at touch. Touch at the end of Sylvia's life meant to BJ that she really loved me, that she really trusted me.

The Living really wanted and needed to touch the Dying as much and as often as possible if the Dying could tolerate it. Some of the Dying are very sensitive to any kind of touch, so it is best to check to see if the Dying experiences any pain with touch. When touch is not painful, it is usually comforting and loving for both the Living and the Dying.

PROXIMITY AND TIME COMMUNICATE CLOSENESS

Proximity: Being Nearby Simply Feels Better

Stan lived halfway across the country from his dying mother, Sylvia. *As soon as my sister called me and told me that she had renal failure and that they were going to have to make a decision, I got on a plane that afternoon.* As shared above, Stan and his wife, BJ, were with Sylvia as she took her last breath. He wanted to be with her because *it felt right to me and because it was comforting to her that I was there. I'd had a friend ask me, "What does she want from you?" I said, "She just wants me to be there. It makes her feel good."*

Dana wanted to be physically close to her father, Michael, as he lay dying in his hospital bed from a brain tumor. It is where they both wanted to be, as near as possible to each other for as long as possible. *When he had the strength, I was in the crook-of-his-arm kind of thing. You know, not cradled, but like he was a big guy with his arm around you. There was a lot of emotional closeness, and because of that closeness in proximity, I was always on the bed until I got older. As he got sicker, I would stand next to the side of the bed where there was room near his head and neck area and his upper body, and sometimes I would lay my head on the pillow next to him but standing outside the bed, kind of reaching over, and talk to him that way.* For Dana, sitting beside Michael in a chair was not close enough for father-daughter intimacy.

Despite how difficult it is to watch someone you love dying, it is often harder to be far away from the Dying because there will be no second chances to be with them again. Proximity does matter. Closer feels better, even when it is hard to witness the death journey. When the Living can stay close to the Dying, or visit them often, there are more opportunities to connect and to complete their goodbyes.

Time Matters

Especially relevant to the examination of nonverbal communication during end-of-life interactions is the amount of time that is spent with the Dying and the willingness of the Living to give of their time to communicate love and care. Jennifer was at her *husband's side nonstop for the last 72 hours of his life.* Lori sat next to her father and *held his hand for hours at a time.* Lori quit her job to *take care of her ailing parents for two years.* Katherine, a working, single mother with two teenage sons, talked about *the difficulty but importance of spending hours every evening with her dying mother.* One of the most common regrets the Living expressed was not spending enough time with the Dying.

A few words of warning are needed. First, the Living can't force themselves upon the Dying. Ultimately, who they want to see is up to them, but you will never know unless you try. Second, the Living need to watch for signs that the visit is taxing the strength of the Dying and that it is time to end the visit. Third, the caregiver of the

Dying has the power to say who gets to visit the Dying, for how long, and even when the visits may occur. Respect the caregiver's authority; only one person can guard the gate.

Most of the Living acknowledged that the gift of time benefited them as much as the Dying because they wanted to have as much time as possible with the Dying until their time together literally ran out. Time spent together became an unexpected gift.

THE IMPORTANCE OF "STUFF"

Tokens: A Little Something

Dana's father, Michael, wanted to be sure that she knew how important she was to him and wanted her to always have a token of his love and, throughout the years to come, an affirmation of his view of her as a wonderful daughter. Michael gave his daughter a heart necklace with her first diamonds. Dana described her gift and what it meant to her: *It's a little thin gold rope necklace, and then here on the right side are a couple of little diamond chips. I wear it all the time. So, that has the most meaning and most value of almost all my possessions because my father gave it to me so that I could remember him. I have worn it whenever I have something important, ever since I was 12. And back then it was big tests, or it was getting into college, or the SATs, or getting a job when I was 16. You know, I wore it to those interviews. I was able to touch it and think of my dad. I wear it all the time: when I took the GREs, when I was interviewing to go into grad school, and on my wedding day.*

Laura felt that having a possession of her aunt's was a way to carry a part of her aunt's spirit into her life. *There is one thing that I really cherish: this ring was hers. She always wore this. I specifically put it on today. Whenever I do, I mean sometimes I'll just wear it to wear it, but whenever I do something to honor her, I will wear it. Because it has some essence of her. So, I wear it, I touch it, and I play with it.* Sometimes, it seems that tokens of love can have the Dying's energy or spirit still captured in them. The truth is if the Living feels like it does, then it does for them—and what a fortunate gift!

Symbolic Possessions: Perfect Beds and Canned Peaches

Tory told us a story about her "Better Homes and Garden" bed and how it had once been so important to her that it had to remain perfect once she had made it for the day. Her brother Jacob was dying, and the bed became a source of comfort and love instead of a source of pride. *Jacob would always come to lay on my bed 'cause I had the fluffy pillows and the nice comforter. I normally wouldn't let anybody lay on my bed. I'm like, "Don't touch it!" because in the mornings I'd make up my bed, and then I would tell everyone, "No, don't mess it up!" When Jacob was dying, I didn't care. When someone you love is dying, you have a new perspective on life, new priorities. So, I let him lay on my bed. He was laying on the comforter that I worked so hard on that morning. I gave him all the pillows he wanted, I wrapped him in the comforter itself, and I laid there with him.*

Gloria talked about coming full circle with her son Jacob as she fed him his last meal. *Jacob's favorite food is peaches, and he used to love to put the can of peaches in the refrigerator because he couldn't have fresh. I went into the room, and he was just out completely. I said, "I'm here. Do you want something to eat?" "I'll have peaches, Mom. I know there's some in the fridge; Grandma put some." So, I opened a can of peaches. I put 'em in a bowl, but he couldn't see them still. His hand was totally loose. I said, "Jacob, this isn't normal." He goes, "I don't know, Mom. Don't worry about it, just feed me. Please." And I did. I spoon fed him his favorite meal.*

Within moments of finishing his peaches, Jacob had a brain hemorrhage—a result of the chemotherapy treatment he was undergoing for his cancer—that ended his life. Gloria reflected on what it meant to her to feed her son his last meal. *I felt like he was little when I would feed him when he was a baby. I felt good that God allowed me to experience that final moment with him. He even said that he was a little embarrassed that I had to feed him. I said, "I love to feed you." That was a very special moment for me. I guess that's the feeling of being a mom. Motherhood is the good and the bad, the sacrifices. To be able to share this with him was a very strong indication to me that my role is what it should be, that I was there for a reason. My role as a mother was important to him and to me. I thanked God at that time for allowing me to be the one to feed him, to give him his favorite food.*

Tokens of love, perfect beds, and helping the Dying with basic functions, all seem to be about things. We can minimize the importance of "stuff" because people don't want to focus on material things at the end of life. Yet these things are about feeling special or about making the other person feel special. This world can sometimes feel superficial, yet things can hold powerful meanings for people. Tangible objects—held, felt, or seen—can hold great significance for both the Living and the Dying. Things can also keep precious memories alive for the Living in ways that nothing else can. It is powerful to be able to touch a necklace during a test. It is telling to look at a bed and to remember how the perfectly made bed became more perfect when it wrapped up the Dying in comfort and love.

REVELATIONS THROUGH SMELL AND PHYSICAL APPEARANCE

Scents Can Soothe, Aggravate, or Reveal

Aromatherapy is often used at the end of life to bring comfort to the Dying using lavender oils, fragrant candles, or scented diffusers, as Maura's family did during her mother's final weeks of life. She revealed, *My mother's house always smelled good, often seasonal scents or simply her favorite smells; so, it made sense to make sure they were present during her end-of-life journey; it created a tranquil atmosphere for her.*

For others, smells made challenging situations worse. Christopher's mom was always very sensitive to smells, which was exacerbated toward the end of her life. He shared that *whenever it was one of my siblings' or my turn to care for her, we had to make sure that we hadn't eaten garlic, onions, or anything else strong smelling, because it irritated her and made her more uncomfortable.*

As individuals die, their bodies decay. Smell is one indicator of the inevitable deterioration of the body. It is more the change in the smells emanating from the Dying that captures your attention, rather than it necessarily being a bad smell. Andy noticed *one day, I just realized that my wife smelled different—not bad, just different—as she got closer to dying.*

Physical Appearance Reveals

Nonverbal communication can provide the Living with the truth about how far along the Dying are on their death journey. Ryan talks about its impact at the end of life in revealing the truth to both the Living and the Dying. *One of the biggest nonverbal things is simply being able to look at someone in their diminished physical state. Just try to see them. Maybe we're disgusted, maybe we're afraid and we look away, or maybe we're just full of pity. But no one wants to be looked at that way. People, even when they look very good, very attractive, really want to be seen for who they are or who they think they are. And it's that situation even more so in Tere's case with her being ill and looking the part, looking unhealthy, looking like she's dying.* To be real and authentic with his friend, Ryan truly looked and accepted her state of dying. He believed that moment was a true gift for them both.

SUMMARY

Nonverbal communication is meaningful to the Living and Dying because there are so many unspoken ways to communicate what is too hard to say, to reinforce verbal messages, and to connect on a deeper level. It is close to impossible to convincingly communicate positive feelings such as love, trust, or admiration, or for that matter, negative feelings such as contempt or disrespect without the use of nonverbal communication. A first step toward improving relationships is to increase awareness about the power and effects of nonverbal communication. The last step in a "good" goodbye is likely to be an unspoken gesture or touch.

People do *not* believe spoken emotional and relational messages such as "I love you" unless they are accompanied by the appropriate nonverbal facial expressions, eye behavior, body movement, and voice. When in doubt, people trust nonverbal communication over the spoken word. Words can lie, but the face, body, and voice express feelings directly. The Living believed and relied upon nonverbal communication to reveal the truth and to express for them what was too difficult to say adequately. And when all else fails between loved ones, the simple connection of touch and gaze signal what we mean to each other.

For the Living, many stated that touch felt more important than other types of nonverbal communication, in some cases, even more important than talk. Specifically, they noticed the type of touch, the frequency, and how long the touch lasted; and they felt the peace and comfort that came with the touch. Touch was a very intimate way to communicate many things: love, connection, and even the sense of impending loss that both the Living and the Dying were experiencing. For many it is easier to communicate all the intensities of these feelings through touch because words simply are not enough to describe everything that is being felt or thought at the end of life.

TIPS FOR BETTER CONVERSATIONS

- Be nearby. Being physically close to the Dying is a powerful message of love as well as an indicator that you are open to participating in conversations without pressuring the Dying to do so.
- Time does matter. The more time that you can spend with the Dying, the more conversations you will have, and ultimately, the more you will gain from the experience. But remember, the Dying get to choose who spends time with them and how much time is enough.
- A touch, a look, a sound of recognition, can be worth a thousand words. Don't worry about what words to say. Open your heart; your feelings will show.
- Touching at the end of life brings comfort for the Dying and healing for the Living.
- Pay attention to the details such as the material things that have personal meaning, the smells in the room, and even how the Dying's appearance reveals to you where they are on their death journey.
- Trust the nonverbal communication that you experience; it is as real, as powerful, and often as meaningful as spoken words.

part two

FINAL CONVERSATION THEMES

chapter 4

I Love You

My mother did not demonstrate her love for us either verbally or physically when we were growing up because it would "spoil" us. She was a child of the Depression. As an adult she told me less than 10 times that she loved me. After she was diagnosed with cancer, she told me at least once a day she loved me. (Angela)

We were heartened to find that for adults, love is the most frequent message exchanged between the Living and the Dying at the end of life. Among the Living with whom we spoke, 99 percent shared messages of love with the Dying. It turns out that "love is all you need" is not just a nice lyric. Now, our research confirms that love is what connects us in both life and death. Angela's mother shows us that while we hope for a fast and painless death, we also value the opportunity to say a final goodbye and a last heartfelt "I love you."

Messages of love come in all forms. No matter how it is expressed, there should be no doubt remaining about the feeling conveyed. How do you express love? How do you want to receive the message of love? There is not a right or wrong way. The right way for you is the one that feels right and, perhaps most importantly, the way that is *best received* by your loved one. Do you know your partner's language of love? There are many ways to communicate love as the Living and the Dying demonstrate.

LOVING THE DYING IN INTIMATE RELATIONSHIPS

A long-time, intimate couple are so familiar with each other that they can frame their love messages to be easily understood and received. So, it is easier for intimates to send these messages directly, in words or clear gestures. Love messages were largely direct when exchanged by partners who knew each other well.

Giving and Receiving Direct Messages of Love

Almost all the Living told us about the priceless gift of being able to share direct messages of love with the Dying. Grace lost her beloved husband to heart disease. Her husband, Carl, died on Christmas Day while they were at their daughter's house. She caught Carl in her arms as he had a final heart attack. *I was standing by him and caught him in my arms. I looked in his eyes, and I could tell that he was dying. He was gone, just gone. I said, "Oh, I love you, Carl. I love you so much. Don't leave, don't go." But then I said to him, "It's all right if you have to go." I gave him permission. I knew he was gone. I also knew that the hearing apparatus lasts longer than the others. I kept repeating to him that we love him and we were with him. I'm sure that was the last thing he heard. It was very powerful, very moving to me. I felt at peace. I guess what has stayed with me was his ability to accept and to absorb the love messages that I was sending him. I think that gave him a good deal of comfort.*

Many of the Livings' verbal statements of love were supported by nonverbal expressions of affection. For instance, Nikkie shared her last interactions with her husband, Les, as they were staying at a hotel near the hospital where he was to get treatment. Les had awakened *about 2 A.M. and asked me to help him walk to the bathroom. His balance was unstable, so I always worried about him having a fall. We slowly walked over to the restroom; he went to the restroom and then washed up. He looked up at me in the mirror and had this beautiful smile. He then took his comb and decided to comb his hair while smiling and looking directly at me. I said, "Les, you're going back to bed. Why are you combing your hair?" He just continued combing while looking at me through the mirror and smiled. I helped him walk back over to bed, and he asked me to help him roll on his side. I helped him and he said, "Thank you." I said, "I love you." He said, "I love you too." I am not sure what time Les passed in his sleep, but I was a light sleeper, so I know it was a peaceful passing. He passed right next to me, and when I woke at about 7* A.M. *I called his name, and he was unresponsive. His body was lifeless, but I could feel his presence or his spirit in the room. Les was pronounced dead shortly thereafter. I really believe that Les knew that it was time to go, and the image I have of him looking at me through the mirror with that smile gives me peace because he was ready, and he was saying farewell to me. I am grateful to have that as my final vision of him. Being able to say goodbye and letting him know that I loved him and knowing he loved me made it easier.*

The Living wanted to hear love messages from the Dying. For example, William relays his mother's last words with him and his siblings as they gathered by her death bed. *We were all standing around her bedside, and she just looked at each of us individually. She told each of us how much she loved us. That's what sticks with me the most. That, and the look that she gave each of us. It made me feel better, 'cause I knew how much my mom loved each and every one of us. I mean, she literally spent her last breath telling us how much she loved us. The biggest benefit for me is just knowing that the person that you loved got to hear you tell them that for the last time. Knowing that that person was also able to tell you the same thing is also a big benefit of having time for a final goodbye.* If there is any doubt about whether love is felt by one partner for the other, there can be a tremendous amount of emotional uncertainty and longing. Blanca told us why it was important to say the words. *Daddy really loved me. And I really loved him. We were able to be cool on that before he died. People struggle way too much on that issue—but if it's not clear, it hurts for so much longer.*

The message of love expressed to the Dying is often accompanied by a message about the impact that the Dying had on the Living's life. For example, Jeanette's message of love to her grandfather, Weber, expressed love as well as the "why" of love—the influence that he had on her life. *I spent most of the time just sitting there holding his hand and telling him that I loved him. I wanted to tell him how important he was to me because my father left when I was little, and he took that place. He was more than just my grandfather. So, that was one of the biggest things that I wanted to—I just had to—I wanted him to know that he'd been really important in my life. So, I told him that I loved him and that I was going to remember him and everything that he'd ever done for me. I think it was the first time that I got to tell him how much he meant to me.*

Completing the Relationship, Moving Forward

Ellen's husband, Michael, died young, leaving her to raise two young children. She revealed that her final conversations focused on keeping their relationship genuine until the moment of his death and beyond if possible. She repeatedly said that *I loved him, that I would always love him. I really didn't want to live my life without him, but I didn't get to make a choice about it. I would do my very best job to raise our children; I thought it was a privilege to be able to have shared my life with him. I was grateful for the time that we had and to have had his children.*

Ellen emphasized that the message of love had to be clear, leaving no doubts. *I think if you're smart enough of a human being, you actually convey to the person that you love them while it has meaning and while it has emotion. I mean we knew we were going to be separated. I just needed to be able to complete with him and to let him know that I've always loved him and that I always would love him. We should all live as if we all know we're terminal. Because we all are terminal!*

Truly being vulnerable and open to the final conversation experience gives people the opportunity to complete their relationship with the Dying, to focus in particular on what is the most valuable message: love.

PERCEPTION IS REALITY WHEN IT COMES TO LOVE

In some cases, the Living fear that they may never hear the love message they need. The Dying may not be cognizant or conscious any longer, or they simply may have never delivered the love message before they entered the dying process.

Lucia's mother, Engeline, suffered from depression for many years. Engeline's illness had progressed to the point where she was catatonic and was not eating. Lucia would visit her mother and often take walks with her. Once, just shortly before Engeline's death, Lucia "heard" her catatonic mother express her love. Lucia described the event for us: *We were on the walk, she never talked, but I talked anyway. It was kinda like she wasn't really alive, but her body was still there. She wasn't really there; her eyes were vacant. On the walk, she would hold my arm. We got through the corner, and then she grabbed my arm real tightly. She never did that. You know? She just held on. She just looked at me, and then she looked up into a tree and pointed up and—I don't know how she saw it, because she always was looking forward—she pointed up to the tree with the bird on the very top. For me it was just like, for a moment, I have my mom back. She used to really love birds. She used to feed the birds. She used to make her own bread and then run one of us kids outside to feed the birds. Somehow, she saw that bird and she wanted me to see it. That's the part that really touched me. I think it is because prior to this time she wasn't relating. She would be obedient. But she never asked for anything.*

That moment for me was really very special because she had communicated with me. Not only did she see that bird, 'cause I would have missed it—I don't know how she saw it with me there because she's shorter than I am and I was right next to her. So, for me it was almost like divine intervention, quite frankly.

She was sharing the way that she could. She loved me. I think there's an innate desire to experience true love. I think she just needed to have that feeling of when somebody just really, really cares. That life has meaning. Even though it wasn't gonna turn it around and save her life, at that moment, I think it was a way for her to confirm that life did have meaning.

And that's where I think that love element can transcend just about anything if you really, really care about somebody, and I really, really cared about my mom. I think she got that. The only reason I can love like that is because she taught me how, because she loved me. I really did feel nourished. I just felt like I had my mom.

Roxanne's father had dementia and circulation problems for the last years of his life. On her last visit, she was trying to unclench his hand as she was feeding him. She shared this story of his coming back to her for a moment to acknowledge her and to share a message of love with her, as Engeline had shared with her daughter. Roxanne told her father: *"Loosen up your fingers, Daddy." You know, "You're cuttin' off your circulation." And he took my hand and he squeezed it. I knew right then that he knew who I was. He was acknowledging me, whereas everybody else in my family had given up on him. He knew it was me on some level. I think he was tellin'—I know that he was tellin' me—that it's okay. I'm okay. I know who you are, and I love you, and I'm glad you're here.*

Did Roxanne's father really know it was her? The truth is that it doesn't matter. What people perceive *is* their reality. The Living's perceptions will become even more important in the years following the death as they recall those conversations to make sense of the death and their role in the process. Roxanne's and Lucia's perceptions of their interactions with impaired parents brought them comfort as they experienced a rare moment of clarity and love. Remember that both Roxanne and Lucia had interactions with their parents that no other person had been able to have with them in quite a long time. We believe that they did connect with the Dying. All the same, be aware that all we really have is our perceptions of our interactions.

None of us have a video camera in our heads to record every experience. If we did, we would be very surprised to view the file. Almost never do we recall exactly what occurred in every detail. Our brains are set up to experience what is valuable to us, to make sense of it by comparison to past experiences, and to remember that version—our own sense-making version—of the interactions we have. So, what we perceive is colored by our past experiences, biases, and beliefs. Communication is a more complicated process than simply signaling our needs and feelings. Our experiences shape our perceptions, sometimes to meet our own expectations (wishful thinking, some would say) or to perceive another's intentions accurately because we have such depth of experience with them ("good intuition," perhaps).

So, are these last messages of love from the impaired Dying a result of "wishful thinking" or "good intuition" on the part of the Living? We can't say, but you can perceive for yourself.

FINALLY, LOVE EXPRESSED

Love Spoken for the First Time

Lori's father, with whom she had been very close, had died a year earlier than her mother. She cared for her dying mother the entire year after her father's death. Lori and her mother had had a strained relationship for most of their lives. Lori tells us: *She was not a loving person. She was very jealous of me and my dad. And she hated me basically all my life, but I think that she came to understand that I loved them both. Just before she died, she could barely speak. I had always told her I loved her. I told her that a lot, and somehow, she got out, "I love you." It took her about five minutes to do it. But it meant so much to me. It was the first time that she'd said it in so long. It was the first time that I think she ever meant it.* For Lori, it was worth the wait. That priceless memory helped her to put away some of the pain from their relationship.

Messages of love are not always easy to exchange. Some have a much harder time expressing love than others. Understanding where the Dying are coming from can help the Living reach out to them in a way that will be accepted and understood. BJ talked about the importance of telling her dying mother-in-law, Sylvia, how she felt about her. *"You know, Sylvia, you've been an incredible mother-in-law, I'm so lucky. You've never interfered in our lives. You've always been supportive of us even though I know you didn't want me in the beginning. I've come to love you and I know that you love me." And she said, "Absolutely. I feel the same way about you. You've been a great daughter-in-law." She didn't elaborate because she wouldn't ever do that. That just wasn't who she was. She let me tell her how I felt about her, and she then told me how she felt about me the way she could. Thank God, I knew who she was so that I could receive that from her and not say, "Oh, you know, that crabby old woman, she never did say she loved me. She never once in her life told me she loved me." But I knew she loved me. What she said was enough, you know; she didn't have to say the word* l-o-v-e. BJ understood from the reciprocity of her words—"I feel the same way about you"—that Silvia meant to send her a love message.

As All Else Fades . . . Love Becomes All

Sandra came from a very traditional Hispanic family in which men were macho and rarely revealed their feelings to others. Perhaps that is why her last interaction with her surrogate grandfather was so powerful for her. Rudy, at 85, had lived a long life and had a long and loving marriage. He was dying of leukemia and gathered members of his family for this message of love: *"I have to say this. I have to let this out. You know when you go through life, there's so many things you can go through, but when it comes down to it, the most important part is having somebody to share it with. Because when you are at the point where I'm at—and you can't even get up and go to the restroom by yourself, and you can't feed yourself, and you can't change yourself, and you can't wipe yourself—I don't know how I would've made it without Alice.*

"I want you to know something—you should always appreciate everybody in your life. But at the same time, I know that school is important and work and everything else, but don't get caught up in the routine. Let yourself love somebody because that's the most important part of life. I've been through a lot of things, but the most important part of my life is loving the person I'm with, and the most difficult part is sharing this part with them."

All of us had tears running down our faces. I think that's the first time that he's actually said that in front of his wife and thanked her. And Grandma—tears were just running down her eyes. He told us, "I wish y'all the best of luck, and whatever happens just remember that the most important person is the person that's there until the end. That's the most important person in your life."

This message of love took on extra value because it came from a man who was not accustomed to talking about such personal matters to anyone. Rudy's impending death had removed any barriers to intimacy and to expressing his love for his wife and family. He wanted his family—the young and old—to learn from his life and to hear his thoughts on love. Nothing but love mattered to him any longer. Sandra was not used to seeing this kind of emotion from a man who had lived his life according to the cultural norms of machismo.

Similarly, Patti's father, Joe, talked about his love and marriage with his wife of 50 years. Patti described her father's eyes sparkling, talking about true love, and reminiscing about the time that he and her mother first met. *When he was winding down from his excitement of talking about his sweetheart, he told us, "I am one lucky man. Not many men on this earth can say that they've done everything that they wanted to do. Not many men have been as loved as I have been." And he told us he was ready to die. He said, "I have lived a whole life. There's nothing else that I would like to do except spend more time with you. But just know that I'm a happy man."*

He told me he loved me. He told me that my husband and I had done a wonderful job raising the kids, that they knew how to love and that was really the most important thing. That made me feel really good. We just sat with him quietly. Didn't really say much more. I just told him I loved him and gave him a hug. I looked him in the eyes, and he told me he loved me, that was it. I left that day. A week later he passed.

Laurie needed to tell her father, Raymond, that he had made a difference in her life and that the most important lesson from him was how to love unconditionally. *"Dad, I just want to let you know how really important you've been to me. You have always had such a spiritual influence on me. I really appreciate that you moved around a lot. That, for me, was neat to be able to go to different places and to see different people and to know that the church was always there, and love was always there and that no matter what, we were gonna be okay. Somehow you were able to share and pass on a love for people that's unconditional. No matter who they are or what they've done, they deserve the respect and the love just because they're there." He had an openness and love for people. No matter what their educational status, nothing else matters, as long as they've been honest. He passed that on to me. I thanked him for that. That was so important. Now I have passed it on to my kids; they tell me that.*

What sticks with me is that I knew that he loved me. I don't think there was any question about that. I remember watching him. It was significant to watch him, to talk with him and know that he was declining. I never really worried about that. I knew that there was a path that he had to be on. It was significant that I could watch that path and wonder about it, but I didn't worry about him in that path, that journey to death. And that's significant.

NOTHING MORE TO SAY: A GOOD GOODBYE

Dana was 12 years old when her father was dying. *He knew that he was dying. Realizing and acknowledging the fact that he was dying, he had come to terms with it. He was comfortable with that. He was able to be totally comfortable with me and not hide anything; he didn't have to hide anything or be false at all, because he never knew when the last time would be; there were just lots of hugs and kisses and just lying there next to him. There were a lot of I love yous. "I love you," "I love you," "I love you," back and forth.*

It was a good goodbye because I think the words solidified that really positive, healthy parent-child relationship. They reaffirmed that he's still my dad and I'm still his daughter. That really focused on enhancing the relationship because you couldn't really know when he was going to die. We had to continue maintaining and building the relationship—we did that. Even though most father and daughter conversations don't consist of "I love you" and "I will always remember you," ours were maintaining that strong relationship and keeping it solid.

SUMMARY

That love is a valued message at the end of life is consistent with past research. The Dying often need to and want to share final messages of love with the Living. It is no surprise then that the Living have this same need. At the end of life, people often experience a strengthening of their relationship and an increased sense of connection. Why is this so? The Living and the Dying usually spend more time with one another; they talk more; they make each other a priority in the midst of the chaotic and hectic world. Slowing down and paying more attention to the relationship often leads to a clear benefit: a stronger relationship and a deeper connection.

We can conclude about messages of love that people crave them and prefer them to be sent directly. We all need to know we are loved. The Living want to definitively express their love to the Dying, but they also want to hear a message of love from the Dying. Impending death brings urgency and intensity to the message of love.

The message of love must be explicit, whether verbal or nonverbal: "I love you" or a hug, a kiss, a caress, a look. Implicit messages of love are not reliable enough. Actions may have several meanings. For example, cooking for someone could be a "labor of love," or it could be a job or a duty or a personal pleasure that has little to do with who receives it. We must express love explicitly so that there is no misunderstanding.

The Living have taken the lesson about exchanging messages of love with the Dying into all their relationships. They learned that saying "I love you" to their loved ones is important every day, because no one knows for sure when their last day will be.

TIPS FOR BETTER CONVERSATIONS

- Tell the people you love that you love them. Tell them often. Tell them now. Tell them before time runs out.
- You can't say "I love you" too much to the Dying or, for that matter, to the Living.
- Just because you say "I love you" doesn't mean the receiver will say it back to you. Telling someone that you love them always entails taking a risk and making yourself vulnerable. But without becoming vulnerable, you cannot experience the full gift of love. It's worth the gamble.
- It's okay to express what you feel, especially when all pretense has been stripped away. Never, ever be ashamed to cry over someone you love.
- Death inspires discernment and wisdom. The dying process strips away pettiness and triviality until only love remains. Love, the highest of human emotions, is nurtured to the end. Count on it.

chapter 5

Everyday Talk

It was a wonderful few months in which my father and I sat up all night watching television—his pain medications would keep him awake—and his favorite shows on the History Channel (we shared a love of history) and just talking about everything and nothing really. (Bailey)

When you hear the words *final conversation*, you probably think of deep and intense messages of the sort you don't hear every day. Although some conversations may be, few can maintain that depth for long. Many more concern the mundane, from small talk to common interests, from familial rituals to shared histories.

I'M NOT DEAD YET! CONTINUING THE RELATIONSHIP TO THE END

Ryan had known Tere since he was young. He learned Spanish from her and they stayed close friends. When Ryan was an adult, Tere was diagnosed with cancer. He visited and spoke with Tere as often as he could until her death. On this occasion, Tere, as she often did, had asked about Ryan's life: *"What are you doing now?" And I think the feeling is, you know, Who cares what I'm doing? I could be getting married. And that doesn't matter in the same way that what's going on with her does. But I sort of thought about it, and she's not dead yet. And it mattered tremendously what I was doing, because throughout the time we'd known each other in our life, it mattered what the other was doing. And she's not dead yet. So, it still mattered.*

The Living expected highly intense and important last messages, but many conversations were about the usual topics they'd discussed every day. It was as if the Dying was saying, "I'm not dead yet," so let's continue to live as we always have. Those who agreed to such "normal" conversations knew full well that these everyday moments would not last forever. Cathy noted that most of her conversations with her dying husband, Don, were everyday but more so. *For the most part it was just everyday, but it's like heightened conversations. It's like everyday but intensified. Because you don't know which day is going to be your last.*

Maintaining a relationship relies a great deal on keeping the interaction easy, comfortable, and predictable. Judy spoke with affection about Sam, her stepfather of 58 years. Judy lived at a distance from him and her mother, but their relationship remained comfortable and solid from visit to visit. That didn't change with his last illness. *We just kinda picked up our relationship. We shared an interest in politics and what was going on in the world. We read a lot. The war in Iraq was high on his list of things to be concerned about. He just talked in general about what was happening: How are my kids? What was going on? It wasn't like, I'm here to watch you die.*

Judy's example highlights how easy it can be for people to pick up where they left off—their relationship or their previous conversation—by talking about topics that are comfortable and predictable for the two of them. Topics that have always been easy to talk about are not only enjoyable for both the Dying and the Living, but they are a way to maintain normalcy—to connect in a nonthreatening way. Perhaps these tried-and-true topics are also a way to acknowledge that the Living is making a choice to continue sharing a life with the Dying, rather than simply acting as an observer of the dying process.

Consistent with that idea of living life rather than observing death, the Living told us they cherished the opportunity to live out the remaining days with the Dying as they'd always lived their days. Ryan again speaks of his last visits with Tere. *To me, the time there interacting with her and interacting with Wally, Tere's husband—there's no question of what I should be doing. This is what I should be doing. It's not as mysterious or even so big and profound as you might want it to be. We were all just there. In the morning we ate breakfast; during the day sometimes I would help Wally work on things around the house, or I would talk with Tere. A couple of times we'd take the boat in the river. Other times, we would drive the roads into the hills. Then we would have lunch. Maybe we'd watch a movie. We'd have dinner and go to bed. And that's what everyone does every day. And that was all we were supposed to be doing.*

By interacting as usual, the Living can send a powerful message: You are alive today, I am alive today, and in the end that is all that is important. Quite simply, you matter to me, and this relationship matters to me. What people often take for granted in the normal bustle of life becomes precious when their assumption of life's continuity comes into question.

In general, the Living agreed that everyday messages and interactions served important purposes for both partners in this final dance of relating. Everyday messages include pleasantries between loved ones; shared interests, rituals, and memories; stories about the past or feelings about the present.

Small Talk, Pleasantries, and Simple Joys

Perhaps the most overlooked of our conversational habits are the automatic pleasantries that people use to keep interaction fluid. In these cases, they show respect and care for the Dying, while keeping the relationship easy and safe. Laurie expresses this ease with Raymond, her father. *For me, it's not a problem going in and talking with him. Well, how are you doing today? Here's what we're doing today. Here's what the weather is like today. Just little chit-chat things. Nothing real, real intense. Very relaxed, I think. Sad, but relaxed.*

Dana's conversations with her father demonstrate how the easy, routine, and mundane conversations can act as a way for them to maintain their parent-child relationship until the very end. Still a child when her father died, Dana reported that her dad continued to ask the same sorts of daily questions that most dads ask their daughters in order to maintain some degree of normalcy in their father-daughter banter. *We'd talk about how my day was, and how his day was. And what I had been eating. Had I been working out. Little things. Making sure that*

I'd always done my homework on time. He was always asking about my friends. How were they doing? Dana observed that both she and her dad became more aware of these small gestures as her father's health failed. She felt that the everyday, routine talk served as reminders that the relationship was healthy, even though her dad was fatally ill—indeed, despite that fact. Her dad was dying, but he still wanted her to know that he cared about her life.

Both the Living and Dying are aware that not all messages can or should be profound. Jayne thinks that *you shouldn't feel like you have to have a deep conversation. It's not anybody else's time. It's not time to talk about your extended future. This is your time with them, and you need to take it seriously, 'cause they are not always going to be there.* Most messages that create and maintain relationships are routine, easy, and predictable. It is far too exhausting, stressful, and unrealistic to think that most of our conversations must be profound and memorable—this remains true even at the end of life. Surprisingly, it is often the everyday talk that becomes the most memorable to us simply because it is so frequent in intimate relationships.

Think about a common, easy interaction in your own life, something that you probably take for granted. Now imagine that it is taken away. How do you feel? If snuggles at night with your child ended right now, or if you couldn't share that morning cup of coffee and chit-chat over the paper with your spouse, or if your loved one wasn't there at the end of the day to ask you how your day went, wouldn't you miss it? When the Dying are gone, it will be these communications that are missed because they were regular bonding events. Their absence will become the daily reminder of what has been lost. Relationships are made up of these small, ordinary moments. Our lives would be fairly empty without such small acts of love.

Simple joys may be unspoken love notes during these interactions; the message is carried in the gifts of extra effort and attention. For instance, Susan recalled one special joy that her mother, Molly, appreciated during her final days. *As time went on, we fed her what we could. You know, what appealed to her. She had always had a very small appetite, and it got even smaller. And in the end, she lived on what they called zebra pudding. It's chocolate wafers layered with whipped cream and then iced over with whipped cream. And you slice it on the angle so it looks like a zebra. She loved that.*

Small talk, pleasantries, and simple joys are possible because the two involved in a close relationship know one another in a way that most people cannot. To know each other well enough to ask about a test that day, or to make a favorite dessert, are powerful ways to maintain a relationship because they confirm their mutual knowing. That common knowledge base also includes the activities and interests we have in common.

Shared Interests and Activities

Interests we share can take the attention away from the illness and allow the Dying one to enjoy the simple pleasures of companionship. Darrell had a long and close relationship with his 95-year-old mother, but they did not engage in one last and profound conversation. Instead, they continued to have their normal and routine conversations. *Mother had a very practical mind. We watched the stock market together and had the cocktail as we had for years in the afternoon. And she'd scream about the low or the stock that was not doing well. But there wasn't any big last conversation with Mother; I was simply with her every day, including the day she died.*

Shared passions that connect people at the end of life may confirm a close relationship while there is still time to enjoy it. Jodi and her grandmother shared a passion for art. *I came back from college with my art portfolio. We had fun looking through it and talking about the pieces and what worked and didn't. I was pleasantly surprised and pleased when she liked my favorite one because no one else had liked it.*

Occasionally, especially when age or infirmity brings a cognitive impairment, the Dying may include a loved one in a remembered or fantasized activity. Greg and his grandfather, Albert, loved to go fishing. During one last visit, Albert took him on a virtual fishing trip. And Greg was happy to accompany him. *Sometimes he was off in la-la land, and he wanted you to go with him. So, I did. We sat on the couch for hours fishing. You know, you're casting downstream. He caught it, you get up. He was happy.* An unexpected virtual fishing trip created one last happy memory for Greg.

Routine Interactions, Shared Rituals, and Private Codes

Shared rituals are specific routines with mutually understood meanings. Without preliminaries or negotiations, people can act or converse in the same way they always did. The Living said that they relied on these comfortable ways of interacting. They gave reassurance that the relationship hadn't changed even if the physical well-being of one of them had.

For many people, rituals provide comfort during a stressful time. In Leeann's experience, an old familiar ritual of watching television and sharing a drink together took on new meaning that was profound for her. She explains: *No more could be done for him, so they brought him home from the hospital. After checking to see if he was hungry (he wasn't), she suggested a drink. She had bought her dad's favorite liqueur. The family members gathered to share "a toast to Dad, to life, and to his new adventure."* Leeann then went on to describe the remainder of the night for her and her family: *And then we watched TV that night—his favorite show. We watched and he laughed. He had a really infectious laugh that you'd hear, and even if you didn't think it was funny, you had to laugh. You could hear it throughout the house. It was a really great laugh.*

While reminiscences typically are extended conversations, other mutual memories are so ingrained in the relationship that they can be referred to briefly, in shorthand code between the partners. Private codes are typically brief words, phrases, or behaviors that people use during an interaction to capture the gist of a shared idea without unnecessarily complicated explanations. They include: a shared look, a private term, or anything about which two people have a mutual understanding. The fact that others do not know the secret code makes it more meaningful. Cathy told us of two instances of the private meanings she shared with her husband, Don. In the first case, it was a code expression about family solidarity that she then explained to her daughter. *I passed it down to Christina: "When we hit the wall, we all hit together." I mean these are things to carry on. "When we hit the wall, we will all hit together." (Laughter) And then there was "In 10 years, we will have money." (Laughter). Things that Christina should know, these kinds of things that Don and I shared, to keep that alive.*

Cathy and Don shared a love of music that became part of their private code. Cathy tried to explain: *There was an opera playing; it was just a Saturday, but we had it on the radio. We played it real loud—always. I was cleaning and he was in the back room, and we met in the hallway. I was going to tell him that the soprano sharped—*Don Giovanni. *I know, that means nothing again. But you didn't have to say all that much, I mean, he knew what I was thinking.* The fact that Cathy and Don shared a moment in the hallway by wordlessly acknowledging a flaw in the opera illustrates their mutual and private understanding. The fact that they never actually said a word about the sharp note, but simply looked and smiled in a knowing way, meant to Cathy that they could read each other's minds. Sharing a private code is mind reading in the best sense.

Shared activities, rituals, and private codes serve to maintain relationships. But everyday talk also preserves relationships long after the Dying are gone. Sharing personal and family history preserves the remembered relationship with the Dying for the Living and other members of their network, especially young family members.

Routine interactions were especially important for children because it gave them a sense of normalcy, comfort, and stability during a chaotic time when a loved one (often a parent or sibling) was dying. These routine interactions could include indoor activities such as shared meals, piggyback rides, board games, bedtime stories, bath-time rituals, household chores, and watching movies and television. Outdoor activities might involve camping, fishing, swimming, playing sports, walking, or climbing trees.

Preserving the Relationship for the Future: Shared Memories

Mutual memories were enjoyed, savored, and tucked away to cherish. In addition to the sheer pleasure of sharing memories, the Dying and the Living both got the chance to relive their shared experiences and review their times together. The Living found relief, comfort, and humor in the reminiscences.

Laurie and her mother cherished this particular talk with Raymond (her dad) before his death. *I went up to visit and I remember sitting around the table with my mom and with him. And we were just conversing about the past and remembering things. I don't remember communicating anything particular to him at that time, but I remember the conversation and how critically important it was. That even though he wasn't feeling well and wasn't getting around well, we were able to sit around and relax and just talk about things, especially trips that we'd made and places that we'd lived—just different memories about those kinds of things.*

The Living spoke often about the importance of laughter and humor. Very often these happy talks were about silly things, unimportant at first glance; but they were conversations that not only recalled old memories but created new ones for the Living. At the age of 21, Tory watched her 19-year-old brother die of a brain hemorrhage resulting from the chemotherapy treatment for his cancer. She took every opportunity to be with him and keep his memory alive in her. She recalled one timeless interaction. *Seeing him lay in my bed that day, we'd just kind of lay there and reminisce about our childhood. When he was kid, he would bang his head against the wall or hit the wall and make it seem as though my sister and I were beating him up. You could hear him yelling, "Mom the girls are hitting me, Mom. They won't leave me alone." Our mom would get mad at us; we'd get grounded. We wouldn't be able to watch TV. We were like, "You're getting us in trouble. We're not getting in trouble for nothing. You know, you say we're hitting you; let me hit you now." It was funny because we were laughing about the day that my mom discovered him lying about it all. I mean it's just funny how we just sat there—and it was just for a couple of hours—but it seemed like it was an eternity as we went through the things we did together.*

Tory describes a feeling of time stopping, which is what she desperately wanted to do to prevent his dying. While she couldn't keep this feeling, it returns to her from time to time when she recalls and retells this story. During her interview she began to laugh, and we could see her recapture that moment and its feeling.

These memories not only structured the history of the relationship for the Living but, for some, the sharing of joyous memories also helped to begin healing a troubled relationship. Holland had a difficult relationship with his alcoholic mother Pamela. At times, he felt anger and resentment during their last times together. The exception was a shared happy memory that brought them peace. *We were reliving some fond memories of the river, and she was laughing, and I was laughing. I think it was the first peaceful conversation I had with my mother in six to seven years.*

In a more positive parent-child relationship, Linda used their shared memories to bring humor to the role reversal that age and infirmity bring to the parent-child relationship. But she also makes the point that it was natural and right for her to nurture her father. *You know, "It's okay, Dad. It's okay." I'd say things like, "It's an honor to take care of you. You wiped my butt when I was little." And I would joke with him. And I'd say, "Oh, c'mon. I mean, you must remember you had to wipe my butt when I was little."* Linda demonstrates the fact that humor exchanged during shared memories can also be a way to reduce embarrassment, as well as to lessen the discomfort of challenging situations that are part of the dying time.

CHALLENGES WITH EVERYDAY TALK

Everyday talk served the relationship between the Living and the Dying, maintaining it in the present and preserving it for the future. However, some of the Living found it difficult to engage in everyday talk with the Dying, even though they saw the need.

Avoiding Difficult Conversations

Some of the Living felt that everyday conversation simply took up precious time and energy that could be better used to get to the profound or difficult messages they expected. For instance, Brenda was waiting for the profound message that never came. She missed her "last words" from her grandmother. *I remember very distinctly feeling that everyday talk was problematic during the time that she was getting sicker and sicker. Like, I was waiting for her to give me some kind of words of wisdom or impart some advice to me, and it never happened.*

Others felt that small talk served as a stage on the way to the important issues. Patricia felt that everyday talk served a purpose during her father's progression toward death, but once that stage was past, the communication was on a direct emotional and nonverbal level. *A lot of the uncomfortable issues about him dying were handled by a lot of small talk—avoidance almost of the issues. Everyday talk was just showing that we need to talk.* For Patricia, the everyday talk was necessary to reestablish their relationship, to help them avoid some discomfort, to get to the pure feeling level of their bond and to feel that again before he died.

Coping with Negativity

Some of the Living reported that as illness progressed, the Dying one became more difficult. As Melissa told us, her grandmother just grew more "mean" as she grew sicker. *She got kinda testy when she got sicker. I guess you could say she would get mean more than she used to.* Although these negative feelings could be the result of increasing discomfort, they also may be the outcome of knowing that time was too short to mince words or suffer in silence.

Melissa's example brings up a truth expressed by many of the Living and identified in books about the Dying: most people die the same way that they lived. If the Dying one was crabby and negative when they were healthy, then they were most likely going to be crabby and negative during the dying process. Impending death does not make people sweet just because they expect to be at heaven's gate asking for entrance. People's true personalities are often most evident during everyday talk and routine interactions.

There may be another reason the Dying appear negative. A few of the Living felt that the Dying became more negative in order to force a release of the important messages. In this way, as in others, small talk is functional, even though it may feel like an irritation.

Katherine guessed that this was true for her mother's negativity. *Hard to know. On the one hand I always thought that she was intentionally being so difficult to make us go to that emotional place. Because we would have days where we talked about the weather, we talked about the food, and we watched TV—real surface. And then she would throw these fits. It would force the emotion to come out, as ugly as it was. Although I had been preparing and setting up for it, thinking, "You know, I need to orchestrate this so that we can have this closure on our relationship." But I didn't know how to get us there, so, I would say she did.* It often takes a push to get to the hard places to heal, but the healing is worth it.

Everyday talk is not all positive, not all easy, but it is functional. It serves to lighten the heaviness of Dying, to seal the bond between the Dying and loved ones, and to integrate the experiences they have had in sharing their lives.

GIFTS FROM EVERYDAY TALK

Cementing the Bond

Most of the examples mentioned earlier in the chapter make the case that one of the prime purposes for everyday talk in these conversations is to maintain and preserve the relationship between the Living and the Dying, or to heal their damaged relationship. To move too quickly and too exclusively to deep and profound messages would risk changing the nature of the relationship. People know this intuitively. Melissa put it in terms of the family network of relationships. She recognized that it's *all about family and knowing that we weren't gonna treat her any different. Everything was going to be okay, that the family was still gonna be there and do the normal thing.*

Lightening the Load

Many people realized that upbeat messages and humor helped them get through the difficult times. And they report that both the Dying and the Living found peace in lighthearted messages. Philip wanted to be sure *to keep things less stressful, so I would always save the comics from the Sunday paper and read them with my grandpa; even if that was the only interaction we had in that specific sitting, we always started our Sundays reading the comics.*

Erin reports learning *how good it is to laugh sometimes and that laughter could definitely really help when you're struggling through certain things. I remember my cousin Anita was pregnant at the time. She had just gotten married, and her last name was Potts. My grandmother, my mom, and I sat around thinking of names for her baby that would be funny with Potts; it was like Clay Potts, stuff like that. We were being so silly. These conversations just helped me learn that laughter is good.*

Then there were those who could laugh at their own deaths. In this case, it has to be the Dying one to introduce the gallows humor. Leeann reported earlier that her family watched TV and laughed the evening before her father's death. *Then, as the evening came to a close, he said he was ready to go to bed. We pulled him up out of the chair and got him onto the bed and, and he said to me and my sister, "Anyone got any hemlock?"*

Clearly, it is the humor that gets both the Living and the Dying through some of the rough moments. The laughter shared is itself a physical release of the pent-up stress that all participants inevitably feel.

SUMMARY

Everyday messages: those pleasantries and joys, routines, shared interests, activities, and rituals at the end of life serve the same purposes in relationships that they do during healthier days. They are the basic building blocks of relationships and they often become the glue that binds us to each other. They help people make sense of events and their relationships, they highlight the closeness and ease between individuals, and they create and enrich the quality of the relationship. The majority of people's time is socially constructed through ordinary, and at times, mindless activities. If you think about it, ordinary moments comprise the greater part of our relationship interactions. Simply spending time with each other reinforces and acknowledges the importance of these individuals in our lives, thereby cementing our bond with one another, while also lightening the load we feel as we let go of our dying loved one. Spending time together to participate in comforting activities helps us live with the Dying right up until their moment of death, giving us time to create new memories to recall years after our loved one is gone.

As with all things, there can also be a downside to everyday messages. If you use these messages to avoid difficult conversations that may need to occur at the end of life, then consider that perhaps these lighter interactions may build the trust and comfort that could lead to the more demanding conversations. Remember that some everyday messages can feel negative, which is also normal. Not every interaction is pleasant during our daily lives. If you experience negativity, consider the source. Is it fear, is it pain, is it exhaustion, is it the nature of the Dying to be negative? Most people don't change. They act in similar ways at the end of life as they did throughout their lives. In these moments, sometimes we need to be gentle with one another; other times we need to walk away and come back another day to try again. Bad days and good days are a normal part of life.

TIPS FOR BETTER CONVERSATIONS

- Be prepared to start with the little issues—small talk—before you get to the big or profound messages.
- Recognize that everyday talk is what keeps relationships going and will remain in memory long after the Dying one is gone.
- Know that your loved one may be comforted by everyday talk, humor, and reminiscences.
- If we're honest with ourselves, death *is* a part of everyday life. Be true to the nature of the relationship you have created—in all its everyday glory—for as long as it endures.

chapter 6

Taking Care of the Business of Death and Dying

My mother expressed to me how tired she was of being sick and how she did not want me to have to make a decision for her that would put pressure on me. She saved me from having the guilt of ending her life, and I will forever be grateful. (Maddie)

The dying process is not an easy one to go through or to witness; nevertheless, one of the most selfless communication acts that the Dying can do is to directly make their wishes known regarding their care, especially what is to be done and not done leading up to their death. Another helpful conversation with the Dying would address their estate plans and memorial requests. Taking care of the business of death and dying can also include making lists of what needs to get done every month or season, so that the Living may carry on with the business of life. While these final conversations are not the most memorable messages and may be hard for some of the Living to receive, they often are very important for the Dying. The Dying want to feel they have taken care of their loved ones to the best of their ability, while also having their wishes honored.

ASK THEM WHAT THEIR WISHES ARE . . . IF THEY HAVEN'T ALREADY TOLD YOU

When we suggest that the Living ask the Dying what their wishes are at the end of life, we realize that possible questions include a whole array of explicit factors about what kind of care and treatment they want. There are explicit legal documents as well as implicit directives from the Dying to the Living.

Legal End-of-Life Documents

The most explicit set of instructions are known as *advance directives* that are often a part of a *living will*. This legal document details what types of medical treatment the Dying are willing or not willing to endure during their terminal illness. During the end-of-life journey, there may be family members and medical personnel who want to do everything possible to extend the life of the Dying regardless of the quality of life, and that may lead to unnecessary suffering. For the Living, it can relieve family members from the burden and guilt of having to make difficult decisions during moments of stress and grief. It may also alleviate conflict within the family raised by opposing opinions about treatment.

A second type of legal document often needed is a *power of attorney* for medical and financial decisions. Some individuals decide to name one person to handle all their affairs (financial and medical) while others name more than one person so that the responsibility and duties may be shared. This is a personal decision based on who the Dying trust to follow their wishes.

A third legal document is a DNR (Do Not Resuscitate) order that is often included with hospice and hospital stays. This order is also very often accompanied by a clear, easily read card that is placed somewhere very visible in the Dying's living space to avoid any extreme measure being taken to revive or extend the life of someone who is terminally ill or injured. Alternatively, the patient may wear a DNR bracelet. Many choose the latter, as it encourages greater care provider awareness and responsibility. These legal actions can be a hidden gift for family members, which is not truly appreciated until they are faced with a hard decision. For example, Griffin stated that *my parents had everything planned out for their end of life, from a living will that included a DNR decision to a trust agreement, which made everything very straightforward for all of us.*

There are *several warnings* that we should offer about these legal documents: First, they can be rescinded at any time by the subject of the orders. Second, these documents should be reviewed on a regular basis because circumstances and thoughts on these situations may evolve and change over time. Third, such documents are sometimes disregarded because family members disagree with the Dying's stated preferences. Fourth, medical personnel may not know of the existing documents or the Dying's explicit instructions. Legal documents help to ensure that every person can decide exactly what actions they want taken regarding their final healthcare wishes. We all need to better honor the Dying's final wishes and directions.

Informal, Nonbinding End-of-Life Conversations

Unfortunately, many people do not take this formal step of completing legal documents giving explicit final instructions, and simply make their wishes known to their primary caregiver, family members, or doctor. In the absence of legal documents, these wishes may not be honored. But the best way to lay the groundwork for the binding documents is to engage in direct conversations about the Dying's wishes. These are never easy conversations, but they are vitally important for all participants because they provide clarity. Sharia reflected on her conversations with her sister and her own decision to go ahead and make her plans for her eventual death after having a negative experience during the death of her brother. She shared: *My sister and I have always been close. We talked about our own lives and end-of-life choices after my brother's death. Also, I made legal and financial decisions for my own life (and expressed them to my family) after having to deal with his choices.*

Honest Talk About Death and Dying

Not all final wishes are written down; many are simply honest conversations about the illness and what the Dying are physically and emotionally going through. These conversations demonstrate mutual respect, trust, and openness between the Dying and the Living. For instance, Mikki shared: *My mom told me that she needed to tell 20 people about what she was going through before it was normalized for her. That stuck with me. She went right into experimental treatment for her rare cancer, and I would go with her to the treatments, read the protocols, and examine the evidence. We went through it together and talked about it in open and honest ways.*

For others, being open to these conversations about death and dying was a way for the Dying to ask approval from their loved ones to be able to let go and to die peacefully. Nyomi shared that *after numerous lengthy stays in the hospital, my mother opted for hospice care in our home. She explained to me, she was ready for death and not afraid. I told her I loved her enough to let her go and she needed to move on; it was truly okay to do so. She acknowledged me with a head movement and her eyes. She died peacefully the next morning.* Similarly, Juan revealed that his father *asked me permission to give up fighting. He asked if it was selfish to not want to fight anymore. I told him that if I was in his place, I would not want to fight anymore either. He died less than two days later.*

By candidly talking about dying, some of the Living realized the toll that staying alive was taking on their loved one. For instance, Sondra recalled that once her husband made it clear that he was in pain, it was easier to let him go. He told her, *"I don't want to be in pain. Living in pain is not fun. It's not my idea of life." I think it was a relief when he did pass away because he was in so much intense pain those last 36 hours.* Jude disclosed that his father's frankness by *constantly talking about how he was going to die . . . made his death a type of relief. I was able to have a better understanding of what my father was experiencing and what his final wishes were.* And Cait affirmed that these talks about death and dying *gave me an understanding that she was going out on her own terms, and was at peace with her situation and was confident in what she believed in.*

Other individuals were concerned that their loved ones would think that they failed in some way by dying. Specifically, Isabel shared that while she was caring for her mother at the end of her life, her mother asked her *whether I would be disappointed if she died. I knew she was spiritually okay. She had resolved all her questions, so I simply told her that I was always proud of her and that I would miss her terribly but would not be "disappointed."* Some of the Dying are rightfully afraid of dying and asked for help to let go. Gabriella shared *he had asked me to help him die months earlier. He said, "Your mother won't be able to do it, and I'm afraid it will be too hard for me to let go. I need you to help me let go." It was one of the most painful and most complimentary comments I've ever had. So, after months of doctor's visits, chemo, radiation trips, and hospital stays, the time came. I stretched out next to him as he labored to take each breath and spoke to him about our conversations earlier about eternity and letting go. He was right; he needed someone to comfort him and let him know it was OK, that we would be fine, and he would also. I wiped his face as he struggled for each breath and he finally relaxed, smiled into my eyes. He wasn't able to talk but tried to tell me something. I think it was "thank you" and "I love you." Then he just relaxed and was gone.* Participating in open and honest talks about death and dying can be challenging but also truly rewarding and a testament to the trust that they have in the Living.

WHEN IT'S TIME FOR HOSPICE

Hospice offers help to the Dying, trying to ensure that their death is as free from pain and suffering as possible. Hospice focuses on palliative care, which tends to the whole person, emphasizing pain relief as opposed to focusing on treatment of the disease. Did you know that people who enter hospice tend to live eight days longer than non-hospice patients? People don't talk about it much, but it's true.

Hospice provides medical support by nurses and personal support with care by trained aides. Hospice offers spiritual aid through its chaplains, and respite for the Living through volunteers who can be with the Dying while the Living rest or run errands. Hospice social workers can mediate to obtain hospital equipment for the home and can look for additional ways to care for the family.

Hospice encourages open and honest conversations between the Dying and the Living. Communication is an important tool for relieving suffering. Communication begins with the intake assessment of the Dying, continues openly and honestly throughout the dying journey, and ends with the hospice staff ensuring that the Living are supported immediately following the death. Communication is the constant thread that runs throughout the hospice process.

The Dying who are ready for hospice will be assessed by medical personnel who ask a series of questions about their wishes for final care, out loud and in front of witnesses—usually the main caregiver and other family members. The intake process for hospice is vitally important because it ensures that both the Dying and the Living are on the same page regarding care at the end of life. Maureen was witness to the intake process for both her mother, Pat, and again many years later for her father-in-law, David. Witnessing the questioning from the hospice nurse during the intake interview, and listening to her mother's verbal and nonverbal responses, was difficult and emotional. *Specifically, it was difficult because I wasn't ready to hear my mom acknowledge and accept that she was dying, and that the only care that she wanted was palliative. It was emotional because I had to face the ugly truth that my mom was dying, that I wasn't ready to let her go, and that I had no control over the process that was happening in front of me. We all finally understood her explicit final wishes for her care, we accepted that this was her decision, and we realized that she had just taken a big burden off our shoulders. There would be no conflict about what to do or not do. We as a family could turn our focus to making her comfortable and to spending as much time with her as possible. We had just taken the first step toward learning how to let her go when the time came. It was a blessing that we didn't understand yet.*

Fifteen years later, when it was time for her father-in-law to go into hospice, Maureen was there with her mother-in-law, Liliane, who held her husband's Power of Attorney, and her father-in-law, David, who could no longer answer questions due to his terminal illness of Lewy body dementia. This time around, she felt more prepared, at peace, and confident that hospice was what they both needed. David needed more expert care, and Liliane needed more support with David's caregiving and for her well-being. *I felt prepared because of my previous experience with my own mother and because of my expertise on death and dying, so I wanted to help Liliane during the intake process. I was able to answer some of the questions from the hospice nurse concerning David's health and physical abilities. I was glad to be there because I realized that my mother-in-law was too close to the situation to see some of the things that she was having to do for David (for example, having to put a thickening agent in his liquids to help him avoid choking and the frequency of his falls). I felt at peace, because I knew it was time for hospice to come in to give all the services available to help my in-laws cope with the situation. I felt confident that hospice was going to make a tremendous difference in David's final months as well as in Liliane's quality of life. Liliane would finally have dependable and consistent help with David's care, but there would now be a focus on her welfare as well.* To this day, Liliane sings hospice's praises for all that they did for both of them during that last, very challenging year. Liliane was also more prepared to let her beloved David go at the end of his long death journey.

MEMORIAL WISHES

Memorial wishes are explicit statements about the Dying's wishes for what happens after their death. Specifically, they mentioned two types of wishes: what they'd like done with their deceased bodies (e.g., cremation, burial, and even a request to leave their body to science), and the type of funeral, memorial service, or celebration of life that they'd prefer. Taylor explained that her dad *shared his wishes for cremation with me and my sisters and my mom. He described that he thought burial would be awful, with those creepy crawly things going through one's body. This is in strict opposition to the beliefs of his religion, and he wrote out his wishes and showed them to us. He knew no one would believe him except us and was thinking of trying to save us from the difficulty of persuading his fellow church members of his wishes.*

Maureen's father, Tom, *wanted to be cremated and asked that his ashes be spread in the ocean on Long Island Sound where he had spread the ashes of his beloved wife, Pat, two decades earlier, and he wanted some of his ashes spread in Arizona where he had lived for the last seven decades.* Both requests were honored.

Sondra's husband revealed that he wanted to be buried even though *cremation was something that had been done through generations in his family. He had buried his father and wanted to be buried as well.*

A few of the Living even managed to find the humor in having to deal with the macabre. Emily recalls a time with her best friend near the end of her life. *I said to Jeanette, "You wanted to tell the doctor something." She looked; I said: "Your body." (laughing) She says, "Oh, yeah." She says, "Doctor, I want to see about giving my body to science." And he got all flustered. And, of course, it just tickled the two of us to death. We were just about to come unglued, because of his reaction. And he says, "Uh, mmm, uh, mm, uh." She says, "Well, what's the matter? Do you have too many?" He says, "Yes, Ma'am. We do. We have all the cadavers that we can handle." (laughing) But, he says, "I would suggest that in San Antonio, that you do it there." Which she did.* Others were not only specific about what they wanted done with their body, but also what type of marker they wanted to mark the spot of their burial.

No Weeping Angels

In some instances, the Living who knew that they had limited time with the Dying would ask about the Dying's wishes. This was the case for Jack, who traveled far to spend time with his dying mother, and felt he had no time to lose. *I said, "Mom, when you die, what do you want?" "I want to be cremated like your dad was." "What do you want me to do with your ashes?" "Put them with your dad." And they were over east of our house about three hundred yards near a little spring that they like a lot. My dad's ashes were just in a can. They'd just been stuck in the ground for a bit. Nothing real permanent. So, I said, "Yeah, I know where they are. But where exactly?" "Oh, anywhere." I asked, "Why don't you come pick out a spot?" "No, you do it." "Mom, come on." "All right," She was walking with a cane occasionally, so we walked out there and up through the woods through this valley. She walked around, looking around, and wandered back and forth. And said, "Right here." "Okay. That looks like a good spot. That should be easy enough to do." And I put a rock there to mark the spot. That's done. Then I told her that "We'd like to put up a marker here too, for you and Dad." She says, "No. We don't need a marker." "Mom, we'd like to put a marker up." "No. You don't need a marker." "Mom, we'd really like to do it." So, she stopped, and said, "Well, all right. But no pink granite and no weeping angels."*

Please Wear White (and Other Instructions)

Some people have very clear ideas about the service that they want to be held after their deaths, and they share their wishes with the Living. Rueben's mother *wanted everybody to wear white to her funeral because it was a celebration, not a time to mourn.* Beth's father wanted *his celebration of life outside on their ranch. He planned every detail of the celebration, including every reading, some of which was from his own poems; he identified each person that he hoped would do the readings, he chose every hymn and song, and he even chose the type of food that would be served: Texas barbecue following the service.*

Some of the Dying made sure to write their own obituaries. In addition to planning his own celebration of life, Beth's father also wrote his own obituary. *My father was a county lawyer and an excellent writer; he wanted to tell his own story in his own words. We were all so thankful that he made the days following his death much easier than they would have been without his many preparations and planning.* Similarly, Mark's dad was a historian and author; *he wanted to make sure that the historical facts of his life were correct, so he wrote a beautiful and detailed obituary.* Writing his own obituary took the burden of getting it right, and up to his standards, off the shoulders of his family, for which they were very grateful. The only thing that they had to change was the cause of death: *My dad thought that he would die from the same disease that his own father and many other relatives had died from (polycystic kidney disease), but instead he died from Lewy body dementia. Because of the ravages of the disease, my dad hadn't told us that he had written his own obituary. But I knew how organized and detailed my father was, so I searched his computer and there it was. Seeing that he indeed had written his obituary made us all smile because it was so typically him.*

HOUSEKEEPING: TO-DO LISTS

Many of the Dying feel the need to "clean house," that is, to complete the duties of their life and to help their loved ones carry on with these tasks after they are gone. These messages were meant to help the Living handle the details and responsibilities of daily life following their death.

Some of the Living were given directives from the Dying about business matters and other details that would make life easier for the Living after the death. For instance, Cathy credits her husband, Don, for making her very self-sufficient following his death. She shared that he began by saying, *"Cathy, if anything happens," and he took me, he wrote down all the things, like a list of what I am supposed to do, like for the next income tax, and then we went through "Here's what you do in case of potential problems." I think it was a kind of preparation for this other life. I mean, my personal life changed a lot. All the things he took care of, I started taking care of. But it wasn't horrible because he walked me through the transition. He even left me notes to find that would help me complete tasks, like he was still there, like he was in the next room. His conversations were the realization that he was going to die, and he prepared me for that; he helped me to get through it.*

Liliane's husband also left her *very practical and organized lists regarding passwords, how to pay for things, where to find things, timelines for when things had to be done, and instructions for how to do them successfully. The remarkable thing is that he made these lists for me at least two years before he died. Because of his illness, he couldn't do them in the last year and a half prior to his death. I was aware of some of the lists he had—we talked about them when he still had his memory and could talk—but some of them were a surprise. His attention to detail and organization were signs of his love and care for my well-being.*

Others of the Living received specific directions about whom to contact and what to do with the loved one's estate. Laura reported some initial discomfort with this kind of talk. *I really think that her knowledge that she was getting sicker kind of turned into these conversations where we covered kind of new ground that we never covered before, like lists of people to contact or repairmen. You know, where do I keep this list? And who does what, and how can I get a hold of them? Originally, I thought, oh, I just want to blow this off, because this is too spooky. But then I thought, well, she's being practical.* Likewise, Lola, commented on the advantage of having three months to talk about things, such as her mother *describing the hard water problem at their house and how it impacted the washing machine and how grateful she was that her mom taught her how to deal with it!* Finally, Frank's father was concerned with financial arrangements. *He would show me their spreadsheet of everything they own and wanted to tell me what they were worth and how they got their trusts. He'd never talked to me about that exclusively before.*

Some of the Living were relieved by the information and direction given by the Dying because they knew that it was going to make life a little easier for them after the death. Others agreed to participate in the housekeeping talk and tasks to give the Dying some comfort and peace of mind. For instance, Darrell finally felt he needed to put his mother's concerns to rest so they could both move on to enjoy each other's presence. *She said, "Well you bought this house for me, and the car, and I think you ought to sell the house." I said, "Well, Mom, we won't sell the house right away. We'll keep it as long as you need it or keep your things in it and so forth." Then she said, "Let's go over the will again" with her attorney. And we did. Then she said, "Now let's go down and make sure that the banks and the stocks and all that are in the right form." Finally, I said, "Well, we've got all that done, and I think we should just eat and enjoy and watch TV and do the things that we can do."*

SUMMARY

Taking care of the business of death and dying is about the need to attend to the practicalities of the death journey. There is no time or room for mind-reading what the Dying's wishes are for their care-giving at the end of life. Creating a legal living will has never been easier. Anyone can create one with a lawyer while they create their will and testament or living trust. Or you can simply go online (be sure to get one that is for the state of your residence), download one, fill it out, and have it witnessed by a notary public to make it a document that is legal and binding. A living will is important to have in case there is an accident or an unexpected illness where individuals have lost their ability to make these very important decisions for themselves. Having advanced directives takes the burden off family members during times of great stress and heartache. It may be your final gift to loved ones.

Hospice adds a layer of protection and caregiving for both the Dying and the Living. Bringing hospice in at the end of life takes some of the burden from caregivers and helps to ensure that your loved one is given the best possible quality of life for the last days, weeks, or months.

Sharing memorial wishes with loved ones can range from very detailed descriptions of funeral or memorial services to general desires about what is done with the shell of a body after death. The more detailed descriptions your loved one gives, the more you are relieved of the need to guess (at best) or argue (at worst) about the best ways to celebrate, honor, and formally say goodbye to your departed loved one.

To-do lists of things that must keep getting done following the death are practical tools that make your life easier after the Dying is gone. The time of grief following the death of a loved one is often a blur. Any help that is given by the Dying prior to their death is a reminder to you, the Living, that that you are cared for and have been given the support to get through life after the death of your loved one.

TIPS FOR BETTER CONVERSATIONS

For the Dying who wish to make their passing less painful for loved ones:

- Talk about your final wishes with your loved ones; it helps prepare them for what is coming.
- Completing a legal, written advance directive shouldn't be seen as morbid; it is in fact a gift to protect yourself, to honor your wishes, to avoid unnecessary suffering, and it is a gift to your loved ones, removing the burden from them to make decisions for you when they are also experiencing stress and grief.
- Writing down instructions and lists to help your loved ones take care of tasks that need to be done after you are gone is practical and a reminder that you are still assisting them after you are gone.

For the Living who wish to help the Dying complete their final tasks:

- Don't be afraid to bring up these topics if the Dying hasn't brought them up first.
- Following the direction of the Dying's medical doctor, bring hospice on sooner rather than later because it helps create a better death and a good goodbye.

chapter 7

What I Know About You and Why You Want to Know It

He told me that he saw a lot of himself in me. He told me, "Be empathetic with people" and just to listen and be there for people that you love and that need you. He said that I needed to do what was right with my life. (Alexandria)

Identity messages shape how we see ourselves and how we feel about that image. The identity messages that we pay most attention to often come from the most significant relationships in our lives. This is especially true of messages from loved ones at the end of their lives. The timing and circumstances surrounding the message can make it even more memorable. Think about all the positive labels and judgments that you hear over your lifetime. "You are beautiful, smart, strong, athletic, kind, and brave." You will begin to see yourself the same way, and then it becomes your truth. On the other hand, you may hear negative descriptions of you and your behavior. "You are worthless, lazy, fat, stupid, cowardly, and a troublemaker." Words matter; they can set root, grow, and create a self-fulfilling prophecy. You tend to live up—or down—to the expectations set by your parents and important others.

HOW THE DYING CHANGES YOUR VIEW OF YOURSELF

The way you feel about yourself affects your behavior—how you choose to interact with others, as well as what kinds of risks and challenges you are willing to take. Identity messages from the people who are the most important to us have the greatest impact. When the Dying choose to share identity messages with you during a final conversation, it may be the last time that they get to share their impressions about you with you. Aurora summed it up: *Well, it's not like they are going to lie to us when they are this close to judgment day. It is so powerful that they could talk with me about anything, yet they chose to focus on me, to help me be the best me that I can be.*

Strengths and Talents: The Mirror the Dying Holds for the Living

Gloria's 19-year-old son Jacob, who died from complications from his cancer treatments, wanted to be sure to point out her talents and capabilities by helping her realize that they had many similarities. *I think he was a mirror of me, in essence. I didn't realize how much he was like me until these conversations. I guess there was a reaffirmation for me about what I did to help people, what I do as a friend, that it was okay. That's who I am. Because that is who he was. You know, someone could stab him in the back and be ugly to him, and he could pick their friendship, their relationship, right back up. And I'm like that.* Ultimately, Gloria learned something new about herself by observing certain traits in her son.

As a result, Gloria feels that some of her own principles have been strengthened; she sees herself more clearly now. *It's important to say what you feel. To share that emotion at that time. Never be afraid. Never. I don't think I could ever be afraid of anything anymore. Nobody intimidates me. I have no fear. I will always have a part of me gone, always; that part I will never retrieve, ever. My son taught me, he was my teacher as well as the one who learned. For me. He taught me the importance of always saying what you feel.*

One day when they were alone, Jacob shared with his sister Tory what he believed was one of her gifts in this life: *"I'm going to miss the fact that you always have a Band-Aid for my wounds." I stopped. I was like, "I didn't realize that I did anything like that for you." All that time I had thought that I was more needy of him than he was of me. I would always show him my vulnerability more than he would show me his. I guess because he thought he had to be the pillar of strength. He would always say that he was my big-little brother because he was taller than me. So, I think that he really wanted to take on that role. I think that's why it was more meaningful that he said that.* Tory is still being changed by this relationship. *I think I have more to say. I think I share more. I think I love more. I think I'm not as reserved.* Her brother still has a profound effect on who she is, and she wants to carry that message with her for as long as she can.

Jasmine revealed that her mother helped her accept and believe in one of her strengths. *When I saw my mom, I was on the verge of tears because I knew she really was dying, and she said to me, "Why are you crying? You were always the strong one!" which made me a little happy, because I tried to be the strong one, but never really felt that way.* Today, Jasmine takes a lot of pride in her strength and tries to use it when others need her.

Affirmations: Loving Yourself as the Dying Loved You

Affirming messages reveal the value that the Dying had for the Living. These affirmations last long after the Dying are gone and often become an integral part of the Living's self-image and can provide a stable reference point when their self-esteem is being challenged. The Dying's confirmation remains a significant source of the Living's self-esteem.

Ruth recalls vividly her father's message, *"You're wonderful, you're wonderful, you're wonderful." And now, I guess there's a little five-year-old part of me that still thinks that way.* In the same way, Jayne knew from her conversations with her mother that she was loved and worthy of affection because *she always let me know I was really wanted and really cared about.* She later elaborated: *This wasn't going to change because my mother was no longer with me.*

Breanna recalls a history of being teased by her family for being "prissy." She admits that the teasing bothered her, even though she admits she earned the reputation by being particular. But Imogene, her grandmother, defended and soothed her in a way that no one else did. *I don't really wanna see myself as being picky and prissy and this is the way I want it. When I was young, I got this Strawberry Shortcake little sleeping bag for Christmas. All my cousins were sitting on it, and they were video recording us sitting there. I was telling everybody, "Get off my sleeping bag. Get off. You're gonna mess it up. You're gonna ruin it." But, through all that she was always taking up for me. She always said, "Oh, it's okay. Don't worry, you know." I remember telling my mom after she died, I was just like, "Who's going to stick up for me? Who's going to understand me in the way that she understood me?" My mom said something about, "Oh, well, I'm gonna have to be a better mother." I was like, "No, you're a great mother. That's not the point." It's just that she always made me feel better.* Imogene left a hole in Breanna's life that she had to learn to fill for herself. Breanna now defends her rights and character as her grandmother used to do for her.

Advice from the Dying: Words to Grow On

Children's and teens' identity messages included words of advice that would normally be shared over a lifetime. The Dying knew that they would not be around forever, so shared these messages during their final conversations so the Living could hear the advice from them directly. Sierra's mother told her to *stay in school and make good grades. Go to college and get your education.* Jessica's father suggested she *use time wisely. Don't just do it because everyone else is doing it.* Maria's great-uncle told her *to finish school and then worry about getting married and having kids. He knew I was going to be successful, and he was proud of me.*

Toby's dad had suggestions *about what I should do in the future and what I should do with my life. Like what type of job he would want me to have and who he would want me to marry and all that. He told me to just go ahead and do what you want, but just make sure you follow your guidelines and morals. He said that I needed to work on education the most because that will shape my life. He said the better education you have, the farther you go in your life.*

Toby was one of nine children from a large, blended family, whose father died of cancer. His father, Todd, crafted a book for his children with his thoughts on a wide range of issues but particularly focused on messages about identity. Specifically, he wrote: *"My doctors tell me I am a dying man. They say that I have almost no chance of living for the next five years. I am the father of nine small children ranging in age from 12 to 5 as I am diagnosed with metastasized colon cancer. This book is for my children so that they know my great concern for them and the place they and their mother hold in my heart. I want them to know how to find success in this and the next life. Hopefully this book will be a message 'out of the dust' to instruct my children how to achieve all that matters in life."* Each child received a copy of this book, a personal hand-written letter, and an audio recording of a verbal blessing that he gave each child for them to keep, read, and listen to in the years that followed his death.

Claire's uncle Matthew knew that teenagers could hang on to self-doubt and disappointment about their real and imagined failings, so he put a hard stop on her self-derogatory thoughts, and he shared with her a slice of his value system, including self-acceptance, strength, and a deep value for education. She remembers, *I was 17 and my insecurities were about being pretty enough, or too fat, you know? I don't think there's ever been another person that talked to me about that. He goes: "Nobody is going to be as blunt with you as I am. And I hope that you remember what I must tell you. You're killing yourself. You know, I don't think you even have any idea how beautiful you are. Don't you ever get your breasts butchered! Go stand in the mirror right now. Look at yourself. Stop this self-destruction. You have your whole life to live. Look at me! I don't have the rest of my life. And if I can leave you with any of these things: to find happiness in life, and not to spend so much time worrying." I think it just ate him up that he saw so much potential that I couldn't see in myself.*

So, he pointed out the flaws in Claire's self-perceptions and then set her up to take over for him: *"Well, honey, you know you have to be your own best friend. You have to." Those words are so powerful, but it's hard to always follow. I try to. But that was probably the most important because it is something that I have to deal with every day. I could send myself into a frenzy if I allowed myself to, and so I always think: Well, what would Uncle Matthew say? I know what he would say, he would be like, "You're worrying way too much. You're wasting your life away by worrying." And he said, "You know, I was dyslexic. When I was in elementary school, they would tell me I was dumb, and I couldn't read." He said, "Look at me now. I'm a registered nurse. I work in the psychiatric department. And honey, I failed that class three times. I forced myself to read." He said, "So whenever you feel like you can't do something, you have to make up your mind. You must force yourself to do it. Because you're telling yourself you can't do it." I believe that for him it wasn't just about looks—it was about anything that I did. He would, I know, be very angry with me if: number one, I said I can't, and number two, I was embarrassed about something that I should be proud of.* Claire's self-image continued to improve based on the gifts of approval and encouragement that Uncle Matthew gave her.

Many of these identity messages come over time and in small bursts at the end, as happened to Helen. *Our final conversation was not just one conversation. It was a series of small conversations over a period of about a week. A minute to say something here, she'd wake up and just say a few things and then lay back down. She'd say things like, "I want you to go to church" or "you did this well" or "take care of your health."* These conversations were intended to help Helen know herself better but also to satisfy a mother's need to share messages that would continue to affect her beloved daughter.

MATURING A SELF: SEEING THROUGH THEIR EYES

Most people who study human development agree that we develop a sense of self by discovering how others see us. The way the Dying sees, in the fullness of their truth, can change how the Living see themselves. For instance, Victoria describes an emotional exchange between her and her young, dying husband, Kerry: *I screamed at him, "You, you can't die. I can't live without you." I remember that he was still strong enough; he grabbed me by the shoulders and flung me around, and just right in my face were these really gleaming ice-blue eyes and said, "Yes, you can. Yes, you can if you have to, and you will do it well." That was a first.* She said that she grew up at that moment. Victoria has gone on to create an amazing life.

What Would They Do?

Several of the Living used these exact words: in difficult times when I don't know what to do, I ask what my beloved would do. As Tory put it: *If I'm not sure, I'm thinking, What would he have done? What would Jacob have done? What would he have done had he been here? Or I'll talk to him saying, "What do I do? What do I do?"* But Tory doesn't just think of him; she believes she has taken on some of his characteristics. *I just think people look at me now and think I'm a better friend. I'm a better person. I don't lie. I don't think I have as big a heart as he did, but I think I'm working my way to get there.* Tory highlights an important point about identity: we are all growing and evolving, so these talks are likely to continue to influence our personal growth for the rest of our lives.

What Would They Say?

Claire remembers exactly what her Uncle Matthew said: *That saying, "Well, honey, you know you have to be your own best friend. You have to." Those words are so powerful, but yet I don't always follow them, but I try to. That was probably the most important message, because it is something that I have to deal with every day. I could send myself into a frenzy if I allowed myself to, and so I always think, Well, what would Uncle Matthew say? Well, I know what he would say. And if I had to think about a final conversation that was the most important, it would be that. He knew me so well. He knew how I was going to be, how I was going to continue to lack confidence and self-esteem. So, I think that whenever we were together, he was always treating me like a princess or telling me I'm beautiful.* By reflecting on what Matthew would say to her now, Claire is keeping her uncle alive in her heart and mind and keeping him relevant in her daily life.

Seeing Myself Through Their Eyes

Some of the Living revealed things about the reflections of self they found in the Dying. Greg said of his grandfather: *I look inside myself more, to maybe see if God did bless me with just a little piece of him somewhere I could draw that strength from when I needed it.* Laura, a college professor and community activist, spoke of her aunt's pride in her service work: *It was nice to see how she saw me. I think almost all of her friends and most of her family do some sort of service or community work. Mom's a nurse; my sister worked in nonprofit teaching. So, it was nice to see how she saw me through her eyes. She was very, very proud of all the education that I had received. She was just really proud of her family. So, it was nice to be seen in those ways.*

Seeing self through the loved one's eyes is the primary way we not only develop a self but change and adjust that self throughout life. The roles we play, though, often change with the demands made upon us. We have children, so we become parents. Sometimes, as the Dying become less capable of filling their roles, we take over the tasks of that role for them.

SWITCHING ROLES WITH THE DYING: "WHO'S THE PARENT NOW?"

As their bodies failed, the Dying's children are often called upon to nurture them. Although this is not the only kind of role-switching, it is quite common. A sibling can become "the strong one" or a mother becomes the "out-of-control one." But most often, the parenting roles are switched. If you have this experience, remember that this kind of role-switching allows each party to experience the other from a different position. This not only gives insight into your loved one, but more confidence in your own abilities to do what you aren't used to doing.

I Became the Parent

At 46, Katherine was telling her difficult mother goodbye and found that it called for more than she bargained for. But she also found that she came to some peace with her mother as a result. *So those last days when I could talk to her, I pretty much mothered her in the same way that you would mother a two-year-old that was irrationally afraid of the monsters under the bed. Because you can't logically talk them out of that. You just have to comfort them. That was my assignment. I'm very glad now. There was a strength gained by it that I don't know how you would get it any other way except mothering a child, I suppose. You know, it's very similar to that. Hard, you know. It's not fun. But that's what we did.*

She Didn't Have to Be My Mother Anymore

For Susan, this process meant that she was finally an adult in her mother's eyes. *She didn't have to be my mother anymore, she didn't have to be in charge, and she didn't have to tell me how to respond or what to do. She finally saw me as an adult. I was almost 50 by then, but, oh well, better late than never (laughing). I just kind of became the mother. Without taking away her dignity, I could be loving and gentle with her.*

ACCEPTING SELF AND PURSUING LIFE

We will hear more about this purpose in Chapter 13; some of the Living who share their stories in this chapter will continue their stories there. For now, it is enough to understand that final conversations helped the Living look at themselves clearly and accept some truths about what they wanted. That hard look at self either confirmed what they were doing or led them in a different direction.

Confirmation of Your Beliefs

Mandy said goodbye to her grandfather and says of their final conversations: *It confirms how you feel. It's him acknowledging back at me. It makes me feel like he knows that I love him. And he just acknowledged it by shaking his head. It just made me more the person I am. It makes me a huge family person. It just confirmed that that's what's important to me.*

George and his mother's final conversation allowed him to *thank her for all the things that she did for me, especially believing in me, accepting my decision not to go into law and to follow my own path.* For many people it is heartening to have the Dying confirm that they made the right decision, following their own intuition and life choices.

Change in Direction

Emily lost a best friend at 50 but gained a new vocation. *Everyone needs to have these conversations. She needed it to go on to her other life. I needed it to survive. In a small way perhaps, to help somebody else as a hospice volunteer in the future. She used to say that if I can help one other human being by taking this chemo treatment, it'll be worthwhile. She looked at it in that manner. I wished that we had a hospice back then so that she could've had more assistance with her death than I could give her. Her death made me really want to take the hospice training.* Years later, Emily did find that training and her passion for working with the Dying.

Overall, knowing that you are appreciated for your uniqueness is sufficient payoff for having final conversations. And for some these conversations bring new and clearer self-awareness about their life path.

SUMMARY

The Living discovered a great deal about themselves from the Dying. Some become aware of strengths and talents that they hadn't recognized or appreciated yet, while others became mindful of weaknesses that they had to overcome. Many individuals remembered messages of encouragement, admiration, and unconditional love from the Dying and incorporated that feedback into their own self-talk and self-image. A few individuals made a habit of asking themselves what the Dying would do or say in certain situations, which gave them clarity and confidence in their decisions.

TIPS FOR BETTER CONVERSATIONS

- Not everyone will find that final conversations lead to dramatic identity shifts or self-discovery. You can't force a particular topic on the Dying, nor can you count on getting exactly what you want or expect from them.
- When someone you love and trust tells you about yourself, we recommend that you listen to them.
- Your dying loved one can influence you greatly. If they choose to use this precious terminal time to share an identity message with you, it is out of love and a desire for you to see and be your best self.
- Be open to what the Dying shares with you. You are fortunate to be in the presence of someone who does not have to be careful about what they say. They can tell you some truths about you,

about your potential, about your life. Listen. Take it in. Decide what you want to do with it.

- Paraphrase what you have heard or understood the Dying to say. Listen for any correction or addition they may have. You may not have a second chance to get this feedback, so be sure you have received it correctly. Try not to change their words to suit your needs, but really hear their intention. Others close to you can often see you more accurately than you can see yourself.
- Give yourself time to take in what you receive, whether it confirms what you already know or offers a new perspective on who you are. You don't have to decide today how you want to use this or what it means for you. If it is news to you, it will take time to really receive it and decide what it means for your life.
- You may not even realize that one or more of your conversations with the Dying was an identity-focused message, until later reflection when the importance of the message becomes clearer and more meaningful to you. Consider keeping a journal of the high points of your final conversations that you can consult when the grief has abated. Accept and embrace it when the reflection finally hits you; sometimes these messages are waiting in our memories for the right moment to reveal themselves.
- Remember that it is a gift to learn, to clearly see, and to love yourself as the Dying did.

chapter 8

Grace Happens: Spiritual Messages

My grandmother was so excited about leaving this earth and going to heaven. She let us all know how ready she was. And I have never seen anyone so prepared to meet God. She was always telling us how beautiful heaven is and that we will all be together again. She was smiling when she took her last breath. (Robbie)

God, faith, and the meaning of life come up a lot in conversations near death. When people are out of hope, they pray for miracles and look for answers. When people are confronted with a terminal illness, they often search for meaning by exploring their religious and spiritual beliefs. The Living want to ease the suffering of the Dying as well as their own anguish, so many pray and share their own spiritual and religious beliefs. When medical science offers no hope, spirituality may soothe as death approaches.

Grace is a positive encounter with a transcendent reality. Witnessing religious faith up until the moment of death, sharing spiritual beliefs in the final weeks of life, and having spiritual experiences together, are all moments of "grace." Approximately two-thirds of the Living said that religious/spiritual issues (hereafter: spiritual messages) were part of their final conversations. Spiritual messages were sometimes brief comments during many different topics, but many times they were the focus of the entire conversation. Overall, people who spoke about spiritual topics with the Dying felt comforted, connected, and confirmed in their beliefs.

WITNESSING FAITH

Testimony from the Dying

Declarations of faith from the Dying gave the Living comfort, reassurance, and strength in their own faith. Karen recalled that the most profound final conversation she and her father shared concerned his unwavering faith in Jesus and an afterlife. *The most profound thing was his declaration. He said, "You don't need to worry about me." I remember him pointing upward, and saying, "I'm going to heaven. Jesus is my savior, and he is yours too. And don't you ever forget it. I'm going to heaven and I'm going to be fine." It was so profound for him and so real for him at that moment. He was about to claim the victory and he wanted us to know. He was ready and unafraid. I think that was his final and most important opportunity to be a witness to his faith, to his family. It was such a strong declaration; it was very intentional and very purposeful. It has had a big impact on my faith and my spirituality. It really made the promise of salvation so real. It was very comforting to see the way my father handled it. He was so sure and confident.* Karen's story demonstrates how spiritual messages give comfort to the Living and often confirm their faith. This type of conversation may also securely place the Living on their own personal path of faith.

Lori had a close relationship with her father throughout his life, but at the end it had been very difficult. She talked about the importance of this conversation because it revealed her father's belief in God and in her. *During our last conversations, he always told me to trust in God, and to believe in myself, and to know that no matter what happened, I'd be okay, that I'd be blessed. He always had a lot of words of comfort, and often God was a big part of the comfort.*

Testimony from the Living

Gloria's son, Jacob, was diagnosed with leukemia. Within six weeks of his diagnosis he died from a brain hemorrhage caused by chemotherapy treatment. From the very beginning of his terminal illness, Gloria relied upon and talked about her faith with her son and with others. In this example, Gloria employs faith to fight fear. *I knew that I could not show Jacob that I was in fear. When I walked into the hospital everybody was there, and I prayed to God just to give me the strength not to show him that I was scared. When I saw him, he started crying. He goes, "Mom, what am I going to do? I'm scared." I said, " It's okay to be scared. I'm here to help you." I sat in bed and I held him. So, we sat there for a few minutes, just really quiet. He kept holding my hand real tight. And I said, "You know that God is a very powerful part of our lives. I have always tried to teach that to you." He said, "Yes Mom, I know." I said, "So grab ahold of him, Jacob. Grab ahold of him and don't let go. Remember when you were little, you told the bishop, "I'm going to grow up to help Jesus." I said, "Well, grab ahold of it. Jesus is here to help you; don't let go, and don't lose that."* Gloria's demonstration of faith would be vitally important to Jacob's journey and to other members of her family.

Sometimes direct testimonies of faith to the Dying will not work or be welcome. Maureen's mother is one such example. Pat was afraid of dying, as many Dying are, because she didn't know what was going to happen. Was she going to be safe, protected, and still somehow be connected with all of her loved ones after she died? Pat's three daughters are all spiritual, believe in an afterlife, and have faith in a higher power. Pat was not the type of person who would be preached to, and her daughters would never dream of trying to do that. She was a very private person, so she wouldn't talk directly with them about her beliefs or her fears. Pat had a lot of fear about dying. She also began waking up with nightmares during her last few months of life. Her daughters wanted to help ease their mother's fears and suffering, so when they were together—which wasn't often as they lived in different states and would fly in taking turns to care for her—they would occasionally share stories about spiritual occurrences that they had heard about, as well as talk about their belief in guardian angels and in the afterlife. Pat rarely participated in these conversations but would listen in silence. Eventually, Pat asked if everyone had a guardian angel. Yes, they replied. Sometime later, Pat woke up from a horrible nightmare. Maureen shared this interaction: *I put my arms around her and told her that it was a nightmare, and to ask her guardian angel to come protect her, to be with her, and that God wasn't going to let her be hurt again. She asked her guardian angel to protect her, and she went back to a peaceful sleep. From that point on, if Pat woke up with a nightmare, she would ask for protection again. Her nightmares lessened and, over time, stopped altogether.*

Pat lived weeks longer than anyone expected was possible. Her daughters believe that in part, Pat lived until she could work through her fears of what lay on the other side of death. Pat waited to die until she believed that there was an afterlife, and that God was there for her.

Prayers and Hymns at the End of Life

The Dying often need to explore their religious and spiritual belief systems as they search for meaning about life and death. Jarrod went into detail about his conversation with his grandmother on the day that she seemed to be the angriest with God. *We prayed a lot that day. She wanted to pray. We would say the Our Fathers and Hail Marys, but then she was coming up with all these other prayers that I'd never heard her say before. I don't know where she came up with them.* Week after week, Jarrod's grandmother asked him to pray with her during his visit. Being witness to his grandmother's doubts, anger, and search for answers left Jarrod with a strong impression. Observing her anger, witnessing her dedication to prayer, and realizing that she had singled him out to pray with her led him to conclude that God was sending him a direct message through the one person that he might listen to—his beloved grandmother. *I think a lot of it was God talking to me through her, telling me that this was going to be alright, that this is something you're going to have to go through at this stage in your life. And it's just another step that you're gonna have to take to get you closer to Me—which is God. He couldn't tell me directly because I wouldn't have listened to Him. Because I didn't want to listen to Him, I would've blocked Him out. Not that God doesn't mean anything to me, but it was more personal coming through her because of what she meant to me. I think it was the prayers and I think it was the touch.* Jarrod and his grandmother held hands while they prayed together—something else that was different from interactions that they had prior to these conversations.

Mark's younger brother Alan was dying of kidney cancer at 49 years old. The brothers had been founding members of a band for over 25 years. Mark and Alan often communicated more through their music than with words. Mark shared: *Two days before Alan died, his "band family" mates had come to the hospital to say their final goodbyes. Alan was very weak and couldn't speak to them, but he clearly heard them. They wanted him to feel their love. Spontaneously, the band family members began singing a cappella "Amazing Grace."* This song meant a lot to all of them, they had sung this rocking rendition of it at almost every gig that they played together, as well as at family parties and celebrations. Then they sang one more song for Alan, then seeing how tired he was, they left his room to sit in the waiting room area to talk, comfort, and support one another.

EXPERIENCING SPIRIT

The Spiritual Experiences of the Dying

Some of the Living learned through their conversations about spiritual events their loved ones had experienced at some point earlier in their lives but hadn't been revealed until the end. The story often had a profound impact on the Living because of their respect and love for the person telling the story, and because it was counter to how they had made sense of the world prior to their final conversation. For instance, Roy was an 85-year-old retired lawyer who evaluated the world through logic and hard evidence. Roy was also an elder in his church, had a strong faith, and had viewed religion from a traditional perspective most of his adult life. He recounted a story that his mother shared with him during one of their talks that confirmed his faith, expanded his spiritual beliefs, and gave him comfort. Specifically, she told him a story about something that had happened to her 10 years before. The story concerned his father, who had been dead for 25 years, and a sealed door to her bedroom. She had never told this story to anyone before this conversation.

My deceased father walked out of a door in their bedroom. She said, "I know it was him. He came over to me and got me by the arms and lifted me up, and he held me in his arms, and he told me, 'I have been permitted to come see you, and everything is wonderful with me. But I had to come to tell you that I love you. I'm permitted this one visit.'" He held her in his arms and then turned and walked away. She felt him; she saw him; she heard him.

When she told me that story, I knew that she knew that it was true. I'm a rationalist and I'm skeptical. But I knew that she knew that happened. And because she told me it happened, I believe it did. It was meaningful to me because she had chosen to tell me the most important thing that had ever happened to her. She knew that my daddy loved her. She knew that all the time. But this confirmed it for her. I think it has affirmed some other episodes that I had read about and heard my friends talk about. There are things which happen after physical death, or maybe even during physical life, which are things of the spirit and not of the flesh. And that reality may be spiritual and not material.

Roy went on to talk about the fact that this experience with his mother made him more open to the possibilities of the spirit. Thinking about the possibilities for something beyond the rational was heartening to him. While Roy and other people like him were reassured by stories pertaining to spiritual experiences of their loved ones, others talked about witnessing their loved ones during a spiritual event. There were few direct words exchanged between the Dying and the Living in these cases, but the Living reported witnessing a profound scene.

One especially powerful example came from two sisters' observation of their mother's seemingly reconnecting with others who had died before her. Nancy and Mary Jo described an experience that they shared while sitting next to their dying mother. It not only validated their religious beliefs but gave them tremendous comfort because it confirmed for them that their mother was going to heaven.

For seven hours on Monday, Mother—who had not been talking, swallowing, etcetera, since Sunday—with her eyes closed and not recognizing us, opened her eyes, looked up, held her hands up, shook people's hands, hugged people, nodded her head, while saying, "Hi" and smiling. Once she said, "Mama." She even did the motions of taking the Lord's Supper. She took the bread, and chewed, and swallowed, and nodded her head. Then she took the cup of wine, drank it, and swallowed. She was having a wonderful time seeing all those people in heaven. It was truly amazing.

Around 7 P.M. the nurses came in to turn her. When they would touch her, she would hurt and get grounded back to this earth. Nancy and I were holding her, and we started asking her who she saw. And we named all these people, about 25. If she had not seen them, she made no motion at all. If she had seen them, she shook her little head and smiled, eyes closed. She had seen seven of the 25 we named: her mother, my daddy's mother, and her twin brother that died soon after childbirth. After the nurses finished with her, she settled back down. In a little while she began all the motions and 'Hi' again just as I described earlier. It was amazing. Nancy and Mary Jo felt comforted and validated in their beliefs by witnessing their mother's experience at the end of her life.

The Spiritual Experiences of the Living

The Living also gave accounts of their own spiritual experiences near their loved ones' final moments. William recounts a story about the moment of his mother's death. He had just returned home from the hospital. *I remember receiving the phone call from the hospital saying, "Hey, you need to come back up here. Don't rush; your mother's taken a turn for the worse." And I remember just falling to both of my knees. I went limp. But while I hit the ground, I felt a wave come through me. It still gives me the chills now. It was just a wave that picked me up. It just kinda lifted me up. And the thought came through my mind like she was there, saying, "It's going to be okay. You're going to be okay. I'm all right. I'm okay. You're going to be fine. Just pick yourself up." That was the message.*

When I got to the hospital, my brothers and sisters were all outside waiting for each other before we went up. I remember stepping off the elevator, and we didn't know for sure that she had passed. But when I took a step off that elevator, I felt that same energy come through my body and told me, "Okay, you're going to have to face this, and you have to be strong for everybody else around you. You're going to have to be strong." There's no doubt in my mind that it was her; I believe that she took her last breath at the moment that I was first lifted up by that energy. It was her talking to me.

Ali shared her spiritual experience with us as well. *The night before my husband's death, I helped him bathe and was massaging lotion onto his hands. He said that it felt like his "last oiling," and I asked if he was ready. He said yes. We cried and held each other for a very long time before he went to sleep. He woke up at 3 A.M. searching the room for something I could not see. I sat beside him, held his hand, and stroked his hair until he fell back asleep. Shortly after 6 A.M. he awoke again and indicated he wanted something but was too weak to speak. He then smiled, looked at the windows directly behind him, raised his left arm to the window, and was gone. Quietly and peacefully. I knew at that moment that I was in the presence of angels that had come to take my precious husband to his final resting place.*

Betty Lynn had gone to visit her "chosen mother," Ruth, and Ruth's husband CC. When they got there, they found out that CC was dying from wounds suffered from a kick from a horse. Betty Lynn begins her story: *Well, this one weekend—it's as my minister says, a coincidence is God working anonymously. This weekend was full of God working anonymously.*

It was obvious CC was going to die. I was the last one to say goodbye. I went over and I took his hand and said, "See you soon." I said, "It looks like you're in a lot of pain, and we know you're hurting, and I just need you to know that you need to do whatever it is you need to do. And if that's to leave this earth, just know that I'll take care of Ruth; I promise you I'll take care of her." Then just a little bit of a squeeze of his hand and that was about it. A little after 5 A.M., Ruth goes to see him and comes out and she says, "He's not doing well." We had been up most of the night and I was tired, so in the family room there was a recliner and I laid back in the recliner, and I just had my eyes shut. I was hearing other people talk, I was hearing Ruth and Cindy talk, and I was there, but I had my eyes closed. I felt I could see even though my eyes were shut.

Suddenly, I could see the ceiling in the room I was in, and his light came and just settled in on top of me. And I could feel this spirit in me, just a part of me. I wasn't scared. It was just like this was normal. But I'm Church of Christ background: you shouldn't be feeling these things. It didn't bother me. I just laid there, and I smiled, and I said to myself, "CC, it's okay. You can go." And in about 15, 20 minutes of that acceptance, still with my eyes shut, I'm just sitting there smiling and just kinda holding this presence in me, and just saying "It's okay, you can go. You can go." My eyes still shut. I could see it come up above me, and just for a split second, it hovered there, and then it went out the window of the hospital. And within about two minutes, three minutes, I heard 'em call Code Blue. And it was for CC. He was gone.

It was so neat, because he was a part of me for those few seconds and it felt peaceful. It was as if I knew what he was feeling at the time and thinking at the time. He was just thinking, "I got to go." I didn't say it out loud; I just said it in my head to him, to my body, and I said, "It's okay. You can go." But to feel him to come above me and feel that lifting. That was just unbelievable, to see the light go out the window of the hospital. All that was done without a word said. But I knew what was happening, and I wasn't scared, and it wasn't weird. But that sticks with you. That sticks with you when you've had that kind of experience.

Images of Heaven

Talk of heaven and what it would be like came a lot during final conversations for both children and adults. These talks helped create images that would stay with the Living long after their loved one was gone.

Daisy, age five, was dying of leukemia, and she told her brother Devin what heaven looked like. *"If I had to go to heaven I would have a lot of different dresses in heaven, I would have ballet dresses, and my friends who had died would be able to dance together on a golden dance floor." And I said, "No, it was rubies." And she said: "No, no, it was gold." She thought the streets would be gold and there would be lots of ice cream in heaven, lots of ice cream. Honestly, she thought that in heaven she wouldn't hurt anymore. She said that she would like not hurting. Some parts of the conversation scared me just because she was talking about heaven like she knew she was going to die. Other parts gave me peace just because she acted like she thought heaven would be fun.* Devin was grateful to have a picture in his mind about where his little sister was now—safe, happy, and out of pain in heaven.

Victoria's husband also shared a vision of heaven that he was given a few days before he died. *The doctors told us that we just had a few days. That night he woke up at the same time that he had been waking each of the last few nights, and he called me to come over to the bed. He said, "I'm seeing something I need to tell you." He was not particularly drugged. We seemed to be able to manage pain with just my being present. He said, "Let me tell you what I'm seeing and what I want." So, he talked me through this vision. He said, "I'm walking up a mountain, and it's really a beautiful forest, and the air smells really pure and clear of white pines. It smells really good. I'm walking up the trail. The forests are green and the forests are silver. I'm walking through the silver trees hearing the laughter of children. I get to the top of the mountain, and there are stars. I've never seen so many stars." And then he said, "All I have to do is step off into the stars and there is God. But I can't do it. I'm not going to do it. Because I've never told Mark, my best friend, that I love him. I'm not going to do it until I do that."*

Messages and Whispers from Angels and Guides

A few nights before Kerry died, he described a vision of heaven that he was given by his guides as a beautiful mountain and sky. He went on to tell Victoria, his wife, *that as he came back down the mountain, he said that his guides had told him that he would have a job in heaven, that he would be a midwife at death, helping people to cross over. He was also told that Victoria should be doing it from this side, as he would be doing it from heaven. And that whenever anybody was afraid about dying that I was supposed to tell them to ask for Kerry. Then he said, "Oh, this is so cool. I've had such a good life and I'm really excited about what comes next."*

Victoria believed from this interaction that people often need to have someone present to help them cross over. She said that by being fully present with her husband at the end of his life, she felt that his death was made easier for him, but perhaps just as importantly, his death was also made easier for her. Because his death had been so peaceful and she saw that he was ready to go on to the next dimension, it helped her tremendously to deal with her loss in the first weeks following his death. Victoria also became a midwife to death. After her husband's death, she went into private practice as a counselor. One of her major areas of expertise is grief counseling. She has helped many families deal with their own death journeys.

The night before Maureen's mom, Pat, died, she was in a coma. *I sat holding her hand and praying. My sister Colleen was asleep on the couch beside us, and the rest of the house was silent and asleep. I heard fast, high-pitched whispering; I turned around and asked Colleen what she had said. Colleen had not said anything and did not hear the whispering that I had. Again, I turned to my mother, held her hand, and again began to pray. For a second time, I heard the fast, high-pitched whispering. I turned around in time to see Colleen sit straight up and ask me, "That wasn't you?" No, it wasn't. And this time there were two people who heard the whispering around the bed.* Both sisters believe that it was Pat's angels talking with her, telling her that it was okay to let go of the pain, and showing her what heaven looked like so that she would have no fear. Pat died the next afternoon.

SUMMARY

Testimonies of religious faith, discussions about spiritual beliefs, and witnessing spiritual events are all moments of "grace" in life. As grace happens, comfort is shared, and spiritual faith is validated. Comfort is created through prayers, spiritual experiences, and openness to spiritual messages. Spiritual messages removed doubt from the Livings' hearts and minds in a way that only faith—a firm belief in something for which there is no proof—can accomplish. In the end, the Living who experienced spiritual messages came to accept that the body is merely a vessel for the soul; that when the body is used up and can no longer go on, the soul of the Dying is released to experience eternal life.

TIPS FOR BETTER CONVERSATIONS

- Pay attention to the Dying so they may reveal their needs, interests, and fears about death and the afterlife. Your job is to slow down and be quiet enough to read the signals.
- Talking about spiritual messages can be very powerful and often private. Be prepared to find private times.
- Do not preach to the Dying if it is not wanted. It is not your place to testify to someone who is not open to final conversations about spiritual messages.

- Relax your analytical mind and release your fear of the unexplainable—if only for now—so that you can experience grace with the Dying.
- Do not stop the spiritual experience because you don't believe it can happen. Yes, perhaps the Dying is hallucinating, but it also may be that the Dying are more aware and open to extraordinary experiences because they are closer to another reality.
- Accept the message for what it is—a gift from the Dying. If you disagree with their beliefs, this is not the time or place to argue with them. If you agree, then do confirm them.

chapter 9

Healing Damaged Relationships

We were able to talk about a number of things that had been difficult for both of us and were able to find a wonderful comfort and peace with each other. (Peter)

How do you have final conversations with someone who has been mean and miserable to you? Why would you want to be kind, considerate, and forgiving to the Dying, if they had never done so for you? The answer to that is provided by the Living: you do it for you, to move past all of it. Not everyone has a happy, loving, or safe relationship with the Dying. Sometimes the Living are the only family available for the Dying, so they are expected to visit and possibly to become a primary caregiver. This can be a very uncomfortable duty.

Approximately 20 percent of the Living we spoke with had very difficult relationships with the Dying. We were fortunate that they were willing to talk to us given the hurt they had to recall. In some cases, the Living simply faced challenges in a relationship that included both good and bad moments; in others, the Living had a horrific, abusive relationship with the Dying. The latter described past interactions with the Dying filled with criticism, defensiveness, guilt, manipulation, coldness, and even contempt.

These Living described their final conversations as focused primarily on the goal of "cleaning up" the mess that they had been dealing with most of their lives. Yet it is more complicated than that. The Living are looking for ways to let go of their anger and resentment before it is too late. Final conversations give them a way to begin this difficult journey. The process of healing as "cleaning up" may include one or more of four ways to resolve their feelings about the relationship: First, the Living may release negativity by forgiving and accepting their former nemesis. Second, the Living may realize that they have to let go of what they cannot control. Third, the Living may create a new kind of relationship with the Dying. Fourth, the Living may choose to not make things worse than they had been prior to the terminal diagnosis.

RELEASING THE NEGATIVITY

Being the Adult to Clean Up the Damage

Throughout most of her life, Katherine and her mother, Linda, had not had a good relationship. She waited for Linda to be the mother she had wanted. But Katherine learned that as people are dying, they rarely change. We all become limited by our daily routines, by our habitual ways of responding and communicating. As we near death, we know no other way to be. With this realization, Katherine came to see that it was going to be her job to clean up their relationship if she had any hope of coming to a resolution of their relationship.

At the end of her life, Linda continued her tendency to be *"ornery and difficult"* and did not go easily from life. *What she would say, how she would say it—she had less governing of it. In her life she would control it—her sharp tongue and her statements—but as she got more ill, she didn't, and she just would say whatever she wanted to say. We would go back and forth between really tough love with her, really holding boundaries with her, and then the next minute realizing that this is a dying person: we need to be nice. I had a really hard time getting in her face about stuff and holding the line with her. She just totally dominated everything.*

Katherine felt the pull of these conflicting impulses: to hold the line for her own needs and to be "nice" to her difficult, dying mother. *That was very frustrating. I had a lot of anger. I did a lot of talking to friends and processing a lot of my resentment and anger towards her during that time. I think that's what came out of it for me. I cleaned up a lot of my stuff with her by taking care of her during that time when she was as mean as she could be. I became the parent. I parented her through that. She became a little girl emotionally as she went down.*

Because Katherine did not have a positive history with her mother, she had to make a conscious decision about how she wished to say goodbye. *Something else I remember, is saying to myself, "Be here. Don't check out emotionally."*

I would have to say it took me days to get myself ready to tell her that I love her, and that seems like such a weird thing. It probably is just an amazing thing to people who say that all the time before they hang up the telephone. I knew it was my assignment, but it took me weeks of processing and going and not saying it and going home and thinking, "Oh! I didn't do it. I felt a lot of pressure from myself to take care of that, and at the same time, so much resistance to not doing it, not going there.

One evening she was just absolutely throwing a fit when she didn't get her way. She had no strength, but she could throw her dinner tray across the room. She was throwing a fit, and I needed to leave; I needed to get home to my teenage sons. There was just all this guilt and manipulation that she had used all of our lives, only very subtly. I began to talk to her from my emotional place. We want you to feel safe, and we want you to be happy. I was trying to calm her down and list all the things that we were doing to help her. She was ranting about how nobody loved her. It just laid itself out there. I just said, "Mom, I love you dearly. I appreciate everything you've done for me all of my life."

My mother had never told me in my whole life that she loved me. Ever. I spent that last month reassuring her how much my father and I loved her. It took me a long time to be able to say it. It seemed like this huge, big, monster—to go there emotionally with her. But what it ended up being was healing for me. I don't know what she got out of it. I don't even know if she was aware of enough. But I got to tell her that I loved her. I got to thank her for taking care of my children when they were young. It was really hard for me to do that for her—to give to her what she had never given me—I didn't want to do it. I was forced into this place; it just seemed like that was my assignment.

Katherine found strength in this new "assignment," in filling her final nurturing role with her mother. *Going through this with my whole family—not just between her and me, but with my whole family. It changed my definition of what that is: of course she loved me and of course*

I loved her. How silly to spend half my life thinking that there wasn't love between us just because we didn't say the words. That was a lesson I learned.

I think that late, late, late, she told me that she loved me, but not more than once or twice during all that. She didn't know how to receive that. She knew how to cook, and she knew how to clean, and she knew how to go to work, and she knew how to sew, and she gave. I think back on the mothering job that she did. She gave constantly. It wasn't emotional; it was doing; it was the doing. I began to understand why it was so hard for her just to lay there and be. The heaviness of death, which none of us had ever talked about, but it forces your hand to go to this emotional place. You have no choice about it. But you can deny it. It's like this huge thing in the room with you which you're just ignoring.

I think I put down the baggage, anger, and resentment towards my mom that I'd been carrying all my life. I didn't like her very much. Doing for her what I wanted her to do for me cleaned that up. That was the interesting part of that; what cleaned it up was that I did it for her. Katherine, in reversing roles and doing for her mother what her mother never did for her, healed a lot of the anger and resentment she had stored up from the need for mothering. *The other weird thing about that was that I was getting stronger; I was getting bigger as she got smaller. That was the strength that I was getting. It was the first time I'd really dealt with her as an adult, not as her daughter, but as an adult.* Katherine felt a sense of achievement and esteem about these difficult tasks. She felt that: *I was bigger than she was emotionally. I could do it. I could push through my own fear and do it anyway.*

Katherine realized that she had grabbed the opportunity to clean up the mess, while her siblings had not. *Everyone in my family—the three children that she had—suffers from very low self-esteem. I took the opportunity to work out some of this stuff, and they did not. They're old, and they are still beatin' that old drum of, "My mother didn't ever da-de-da." "My parents, my family, didn't ever do this, and that's why I'm so screwed up." I can see that, and I'm hoping that I learned and cleaned up and can move on. I'm hoping that I'm not just carryin' around that trailer full of history of "my family screwed me up."* Not only did she surrender her negativity, but she also opened to receiving love, just as she had asked her mother to do.

The amazing thing is that, after both of my parents were gone, love came back into my life two months later. I didn't know what to do with that, but I thought, this doesn't come around a lot. I'm jumping in with both feet. Well, that's a whole separate kind of story, but I opened myself up to relationships and love in my life.

Stop the Blame Game

Sam described cleaning up the mess in terms of talking about the need for the Living to own their part of the problem and to stop the blame game. Sam revealed: *My dad was the obvious problem person in the family, but the relationship I had the most trouble with was the relationship with my mother. I think what happened with her in those last couple of years was really some closure to my issues with both of them. I remember that scene from* On Golden Pond *where Jane Fonda is cursing about her dad to her mom. And her mom slaps her and says, "That son of a bitch is my husband." You just basically grow up. There comes a point when you can't blame your parents anymore for your life. Her death and being with her leading up to her death kind of brought that to an end for me. I mean that was the end of the blame game; there really was no longer any parental reason for any of my problems. I had to own them myself.*

LETTING GO OF WHAT YOU CANNOT CONTROL

Acknowledging and Forgiving

Holland was angry with his mother, Pamela, for drinking herself to death and for the years when she couldn't be a mom to him and his siblings. On his 16th birthday, he discovered that his mom had been diagnosed with hepatitis C and liver disease. Of course, he wanted to know what she could do about it, and she simply responded that she would die, which she did about four years later. He had known of her alcoholism from a very young age, but she stopped drinking when he was 6 and resumed when he was 12. During that time, he "*got a sense of who she was as a person.*" He loved talking with her until she started drinking again after his stepfather left.

His frustration with his mother is still very real to Holland. He recalls feeling self-righteous in the face of what he saw as her selfishness. *I remember a conversation we had in the truck where it was almost like a parent to a child. I was the parent though. I said, "Why are you doing this?" She replied, "You can't tell me what to do. I will do what I want when I want to do it. You don't have any force in my life." I said, "All you have to do is stop, and you can see me graduate." It wasn't that important to her, so she kept doing it. The doctors, on three separate occasions, gave her less than a year to live. If she didn't stop drinking, less time than that. She repeatedly beat it. She stepped up her drinking and lived another four years. And that's why her death, to this day—I don't believe it. Because she was so stubborn, she thought that she wasn't gonna die.*

Talking with someone who has caused tremendous pain in your life is not easy for anyone, and it doesn't get any easier because someone is dying. The big difference is that the Living feels the urgency to have the talk—the talk has to happen now, before the person is dead. Holland needed a final showdown with his mother and he recalled giving himself a pep talk: *If you're angry, don't show it, don't feel it, 'cause you don't want that to be the last impression she has. I was just talking with her and explaining to her that everything was okay. That she raised me just fine, and that I was the person I am today because of who she made me and the values that she instilled in me in the time we had together when she was sober.*

I knew her biggest fear was dying a failure because she didn't accomplish anything; she hadn't had a job in 23 years. But I was telling her that she succeeded in life through her children, that I am the person I am because of her. There are things that I accomplish because of her. She can find success in my accomplishments. She wasn't a failure in her life because all of us were good people. She doesn't have to fight it anymore. She doesn't have to deal with the pain that she had within her because if she was waiting to die until she had a success, then she could die in peace, because we were her successes. I held her hand and I got to tell her I loved her. She told me she loved me.

The negative effects of Pamela's choices will live on for some time in Holland's life but his final conversation was the beginning of awareness and a shift in his attitude. *At some point in the last conversations, I went from being bitter about what she was telling me to accepting the fact that she wasn't telling me these because she believed 'em; she was telling me all this because it helped her with her reality. If that's what she needed, no matter what, I didn't have to believe it. I refused, and I live my life by my own saying, "I refuse to be a victim of circumstance." My mom was an alcoholic; it doesn't mean I have to be. I don't have to give in to drugs. Too many people I know are victims of circumstance. You can do it if you just set your mind to it. The conversations I had with my mom led to a lot of attitude adjustments within me.*

But in the end, that final night, I wasn't worried about anything she'd taken from me. I was just worried that she knew that it was okay, that despite everything, I loved her. And that's forgiveness. If I learned anything, it's no matter what someone does to you, there's always room for forgiveness.

Holland took a huge leap into the mess of his relationship with Pamela to accept her, acknowledge her alcoholism, and finally to forgive her. In doing so, he prepared himself to heal a lifetime of hurt and disappointment.

Acceptance of One Another's Differences

Victoria and her aging father had often been at odds with each other. They had very different personalities and ways of seeing the world. Victoria had often felt judged by her father. They also had differences in how they would react to things—talking versus silences. During their final conversations, they found a way to acknowledge and accept their different ways of handling things and seeing the world. Victoria said that the transition began when her father first told her about his aneurysm and his grim prognosis. *He said he wanted to try this, and he accepted the possibility of losing, and while I would have made a different decision, I did not disagree with him. He took control of his death. It seemed like he was honoring me in telling me his reasons and not just saying none of your business. I was honoring him by accepting it. Mutual respect was a big deal in my relationship with my father, and that conversation really played it out. I think all the conversations during that time had echoes of that—where we sort of made decisions together along the way.*

Unfortunately, Victoria's father had multiple complications following the risky surgery. *It became clear that he was going to die, and one of the big things about the conversations in the last period was that I had trouble with his long silences when we were younger. I sat in his room and did needlepoint and was finally able to follow his pace and not feel rejected by the silences. That felt very good. The silences weren't because he was sick; I mean, that was just the way the man was. I was very happy that before he died, I had reached an acceptance of that and no longer felt rejected by it. He was very grateful for my being there, my having taken time off from work to be there, my going down and getting him the Wall Street Journal, or the strawberry ice cream that he wanted, all of that stuff during the period when he was doing well. That felt really good to be able to be of help to him. I felt really good that he, even though he made a choice that was different than the choice I would have made to pursue a risky surgery, he did it on his terms. He lived on his terms, died on his terms. Because I went and stayed down there those six weeks and did the deal, I felt peaceful. I did what I could do for him, helped him go out. So, it felt pretty triumphant.*

Releasing the emotional hold that a lifetime of negativity and pain exerts is not easy, but it is possible. The Living who acknowledge, accept, and forgive those who hurt them find freedom and peace.

CREATING A NEW KIND OF RELATIONSHIP WITH THE DYING

Not all family relationships are close, and yet some people find that impending death is the opportunity to set things right and to make a family relationship what they want it to be. Final conversations may be seen as the last chance to get the relationship right. Just because the Living or the Dying want it to be so doesn't mean that it will happen. But it could.

Receiving the Surprise Apology

Sometimes, especially after the Living partner to a difficult relationship has found a way to release some of the pain, they will receive a lovely reward—an apology. Pinky was given that gift from her mother. She would never have received it if she hadn't given her mother something as well. Pinky was caring for her mother, perhaps mostly out of obligation. Despite cultural changes in gender roles, we still expect that mothers will take care of their babies, and more subtly, we still expect that daughters will take care of their dying parents. Pinky was not caring for her mother with the expectation that she would receive an apology; after all, she had never received an apology before. She cared for her because she was supposed to do this job. Pinky begins her story by explaining a little about their relationship.

My mom and I did not get along. My mom beat me, my father beat me, there was a lot of bad karma between my mom and me. But during her final weeks and days, the wall kinda went down. I was busy taking care of her, and her apology came unexpectedly during this time.

My mother had her chair that she sat in. And she'd point to her feet and ask, "Take them off, please." This was not the mother that I grew up with. My mother wasn't this docile kind of a person who would say please, but now she was. She had these special shoes 'cause she'd had some problems with her feet. So, I would take off her shoes and massage her feet—I never massaged anybody's feet—she had these calluses and whatnot. We would look at each other while I massaged her feet—this was not something we did—we didn't get along. But it didn't matter anymore. I would talk to her, just to make conversation to fill the awkward silences. I think it was kind of nervous at one point, and she said something like, "Tell me about your marriage." I remember thinking, she knew something wasn't right. So, I explained to her that it wasn't going well and I cried. She just looked at me and she said, "I'm sorry. I wish things were better; I'm sorry I wasn't a better mother." And that is worth 10,000 days of conversation.

We never had another conversation like that, for the rest of her life or before. That was it. And that more than anything healed whatever was going on prior to that. We did not have a good relationship for a lot of my life, but those simple words, "I'm sorry I wasn't a better mother" made all the difference in the world. My mother was the best mother that she could possibly be, given what she came into the world with. I'm eternally grateful that I had that final conversation. Within a couple days she went into a coma.

In the end, it makes you wonder why saying two simple words—"I'm sorry"—is so difficult for people, especially when there can be so much healing as a result. A message of apology may be long overdue, but it is finally a gift of peace to the Living.

Closing a Door, Opening a Window

Laurel's experience shows that final conversations do not satisfy all of one's wishes but may create something new and unexpected. Laurel described her relationship with her brother, Reed, as one that had never been close but became more alienated with time. *We didn't really hate each other or anything, but I don't ever remember being close with him. But Reed had some—as I was older—some particular kind of grudge or something with me. I don't know to this day really what it was.*

As his illness progressed, he began to get really crotchety. During a visit I noticed more and more that he was picking on me, and I tried to be mature about it, but it became apparent that he was being mean especially to me. Not my sisters, not my mom, or anybody, but it was me. I said one day to him, "I wanna talk." I'd had enough and said, "I wanna talk this out. I don't get why you're mad at me. What is this about?" He said, "Well, we've never been close." And I said, "Well, there's a lot of siblings that aren't close. So what? That's not a big deal. I mean it's one thing not to be close, but I feel like you're being hostile towards me. I think it's unfortunately the case that a lot of siblings never really get close to each other. It's too bad, but it's not something you've never heard of." So, I kinda tried to make that distinction and didn't try to dismiss what he said: that we were not close. "Because I know you're right. I haven't wanted it to be that way, and I don't know why it's that way." He said, "I just, I don't wanna talk to you. Period. I just don't want to." I can't remember what I said, but I just remember how deeply that hurt because it was so final. It was like closing a door.

Surprisingly, a month after her pleas to talk with him, Reed contacted Laurel. *He called, and he said on the phone, "I don't want to talk to you." But he wanted to write his life story, because he knew he wouldn't meet his grandchildren because he wasn't gonna survive it. We didn't know how it would end, so I was just so delighted that he made contact. I'm considered the writer of the family, and so I think that's why he came to me. But maybe it was in a way a sort of an apology, an offering, and I took it. I said, "I'd love to."*

There were weeks when we met daily. I don't think there was a week that we met less than three times. He would talk about his life. I'd record it. I'd prompt him. He's done some neat stuff. He was a metal sculptor. All of a sudden, we were closer than we'd ever been. And I never could ask him what had happened between us because I was just letting it, whatever it was, heal through this process. And it did to a great extent.

As Laurel and Reed demonstrate, some relationships find a way to create a new—and hopefully improved—relationship at the end of life. It may be based on the needs and talents of both rather than duty, so *don't expect it*. It appears to be an unexpected, beautiful gift between the Dying and the Living. Regardless of the reason for the opening, there seems to be a sigh of relief between the Living and the Dying at the shift in the relationship that is experienced. Reed invited a new and different kind of relationship. Although he closed the door firmly on "fixing" the sibling bond, he opened the window by inviting Laurel to join him in forming a new relationship between two creative people, based on their talents.

DON'T MAKE IT WORSE: MAKE YOUR PEACE

Let's say your relationship was not terribly dysfunctional but just irritating enough to fall into the normal range of family spats. Often, the best you can do with a slightly negative, yet not horrible, relationship is to not make it any worse.

Herschel had had his disagreements with his son, Douglas. But now Douglas was dying of cancer, and Herschel knew they needed to talk. *It's a chance to kind of make your peace and say your final goodbye. You want conversations. I guess in most cases, you hope they end well. I would say that most of our conversations at the end of his life were better than some of the conversations earlier when I'd get angry with him about things. So, they didn't end in anger or some other kind of unpleasant emotions. I mean, I wouldn't say it was all pleasant; it certainly wasn't. But I mean at least anger wasn't generally present or saying something that you kind of regretted.*

The Living who had troubled relationships with the Dying talked about the importance of not making things worse with the Dying. A cynic might think that the Living didn't want to add to their own guilt by making the situation worse between the Dying and themselves. Yet, in talking with the Living, we were left with the impression that they genuinely did not want to be any part of more hurt in these relationships. They did what many of us could not—they overcame their own anger and disappointment and did not demand an apology or a reckoning of the Dying one's bad behavior. They risked being hurt again by being vulnerable and open. In their vulnerability, they were able to let go and release their heartache, thereby freeing them to move on without regrets and without the chains of anger and pain that had bound them to the Dying for so long.

SUMMARY

Almost every close relationship can be challenging from time to time. If your relationship with the Dying has not been consistently difficult, you can choose to avoid making things worse by focusing on positive things from your relationship and letting go of past minor grievances. If you have had a very painful relationship with the Dying, you will find models from the Living who showed compassion, forgiveness, and release of negativity. They remind us what the human spirit is capable of accomplishing.

We aren't telling you that you *must* have a final conversation with someone who has hurt you. Each person must decide for themselves what is possible or worth the risk. But some of the Living managed to let go of what they could not control, released their negative feelings, and sometimes created a new kind of relationship in the process. They experienced their final conversations as healing acts. For others, these conversations marked only the beginning of their healing journey. We also understand that there may be those who have had final conversations that resulted in negative outcomes. Since these people understandably chose not to talk with us—because it hurt too much to relive the conversation—we can't say for sure what these conversations were like.

Anger and resentment are not uncommon feelings in families and close relationships. What no one tells us is that these negative emotions often hurt us more than they hurt the person who caused them. Letting go of this pain is the only way to move on to healthier relationships and happier lives. Final conversations at the end of life with the one who has caused the harm is one way for you to begin healing.

TIPS FOR BETTER CONVERSATIONS

- Release the power that anger and resentment have over you by letting go of your baggage with the Dying once and for all.
- Be prepared for negativity. The Dying do not become angels just because they are at death's doorstep. Set some boundaries, if necessary, to protect yourself.
- Be fully present as much as you are able. Feel the emotions you want to express with the Dying. This is your chance to heal.
- Forgive. This decision is the most powerful you can make in the face of hurt and pain. Forgive them so they may let go; forgive them so that you can move on.
- If you think that hard conversations will be too difficult for you or for the Dying, then your healing may have to begin after the Dying is gone. Get help.
- Don't be afraid to work with a grief counselor. Communication in damaged relationships does not heal all wounds—it just begins the healing process for many of the Living.
- Set yourself up to look back with compassion and move forward with no regrets.

part three

TRANSFORMATIONAL EFFECTS OF FINAL CONVERSATIONS

chapter 10

Benefits of Final Conversations

I saw my father every day from the time that he got sick until he finally passed away. I kissed him goodnight before leaving the hospital the day he passed away. Being able to share these final days with him helped me to accept his death. (George)

The more opportunities that the Living had to participate in final conversations with the Dying, the more the Living expressed feelings of acceptance. Conducting this research for over two decades, we know that the Dying can help the Living prepare for their death. We discovered that *acceptance* of the death was a starting point for the Living. Then, after some time and reflection of their conversations, individuals eventually discover some positive outcomes. The time it takes for these to emerge can be months, years, or even decades after the death of their loved ones. Positive outcomes include *closure, coping, and personal growth.* These outcomes emerge only after the grief from the death has eased and the Living have time to reflect on their final conversations. The effects of these conversations emerge in their own time.

The Dying may help the Living begin processing their grief and loss prior to the death. Grief can begin from the moment of a terminal diagnosis. As the Dying come to terms with their own death, they can help frame the end-of-life journey for the Living.

ACCEPTANCE

Acceptance is a critical starting point for the Living to be able to move on following the death of their loved one. Grief following the death is normal, and the Living must process the death of their loved one and the loss that it means to their lives before they are able to begin processing much about their final conversations. Acceptance often comes from recognizing that the Dying will finally be released from their pain.

Recognition and Release of Pain for the Dying

Witnessing the pain that can accompany the dying process is distressing and may give the Living a reason to be able to let go of the Dying. Donald shared, *I felt at peace because I knew that my granddad was in pain during the last few months. Our conversations made me realize that he would feel better afterwards. Of course, I was upset when he passed, but I was at peace knowing that he was in a better place and wasn't hurting anymore.* Petra also shared *that in a lot of our conversations, we discussed her pain. I think that had a lot to do with me feeling a sense of relief after it was all over. I was sad that my mom left, but I was relieved to not see her go through all that every single day.*

The Dying's Acceptance of Their Impending Death

When the Dying reach a point of peace and acceptance about their death, it can help the Living get to the same place of acceptance. Maureen's mother caught her tearing up one afternoon, and she recalls her saying, *"Don't cry for me; I have had a good life. Save the tears for the young mothers who die or for the little ones whose lives are cut short. I was almost killed in a car accident when you were eight years old; I still needed to help your dad raise the six of you. But here I am. I was able to see all of you grow into successful adults with families of your own. I've witnessed 11 grandchildren come into and thrive in this world. How blessed am I? I've accepted this, and it is time for you to do so as well."* This specific conversation was the beginning of acceptance for Maureen.

Kaylin revealed that it was her sister's strength and acceptance of what was to come that helped her siblings and her accept the impending death. *The final conversations I had with my sister changed the whole way I viewed her death. She was always so positive about her situation. Even when the doctors gave her days to live, she stayed positive; she never stopped making jokes to ease the tension. Every time someone would start to get tears in their eyes, she would ask why they were crying and told them there is nothing to be sad about. Her incredible strength to hold herself together those last four months was the reason for the strength the rest of our siblings had after her passing. That was a gift she left us with. Even though there were tears after her death, losing her wasn't unbearable like I had expected.*

Not everyone who is dying reaches the point of acceptance about their death, but for those who do, the Dying create an opening for other positive outcomes to emerge.

CLOSURE

Closure at the end of life is the perception that everything that needed to be said or done between the Living and Dying is complete, leaving no regrets. Closure comes with time—enough time to prepare for the death—whether that is weeks or months or longer. And sufficient time can mean that they were able to say all that they wanted to say.

Nothing Left Unsaid

Final conversations gave individuals what they needed to be able to come to terms with the death of their loved ones. Hank shared: *It gave me a sense of closure. I was able to hear all the things that I wanted and needed to hear before he passed. I was also able to tell him the things I wanted to tell him so that he knows how much he meant to me. I truly believe that he is watching over me to this day, and I still think about him constantly.* Others shared with us very similar messages. For instance, Tara told us, *My mother and I talked about many things which just brought closure to me. This made it a little easier to let her go, and I know that I will see her one day.* We have heard many people express that hearing the Dying's final words is compelling, comforting, and brings closure. Perhaps this is because people believe that someone's last words or actions reveal what was most important to them.

Closure Takes Time

While it is never easy watching a loved one as they are on their death journey, having enough time to ask questions, share stories, and simply be together seems to be a big part of the closure. As Gabbie noted, *it calmed me. We were able to talk about the future, and the time we had allowed us to come to terms with his passing.*

For some, it was about the amount of time they had to process what was happening. Jaime told us, *The fact that we had a year to watch my granddad die was brutal, but with that timeline came a sense of closure, having faced the reality that death was near and inevitable.* Others talked about the frequency and consistency of their interactions. Eric said that *it was easier to accept the death because I was able to see the person at least once a week up until their death.*

Many people live in different parts of the country, limiting their opportunities for face-to-face interactions. When Colin heard that his dad was in home hospice, he *immediately went to his house for a week. There is not much else to do there, other than talk and watch TV, but we spent a lot of time together. I left to return home, with the intent of coming back with my wife and kids, so they could say goodbye. My dad died days after I left. I feel that the timing was good for me, because we were able to talk, but I wish my wife and kids could have said goodbye. I felt I had closure, so it made his death easier to deal with, but still hard.*

Death of a loved one is always hard, but *not* having the opportunity to say goodbye, *not* reaching a sense of closure, is harder in the long run. While it would have been wonderful if Colin's wife and children could have said goodbye, it was most important for him to have this time with his dad to prepare himself for the death and to have his closure. Colin's wife and children can get some closure from the stories that he shares with them from that week and from his memories about his dad. The benefits of final conversations can be shared with others by telling them about the conversations.

COPING

One benefit of talking with the Dying is that they have the opportunity to help the Living cope with their death. Specifically, if the

Living doesn't shut down talk about dying, then the Dying may describe and explain their understanding of their death journey to the Living. These conversations may reveal to the Living what the Dying are going through physically, emotionally, spiritually, and psychologically. The goal of having open communication between the Dying and the Living is to help prepare both for what is to come and to help figure out what can best be done to ease the process.

Your ability to participate in authentic and honest communication depends on your readiness. Try asking yourself the following questions. First, how comfortable are you, your family members, and the Dying with expressing and receiving distressing emotions, such as fear, sadness, and even anger, that often are present at the end of life? Second, can you initiate conversations from the easy to the more challenging ones? (If you are unsure, see Chapter 16 for help.) Third, are you willing to share information honestly and fully with one another? Fourth, can the Dying and the Living agree on who will make end-of-life decisions, and are all involved parties willing to accept them? Fifth and finally, does everyone know what they wish to say and how to best say it? If the Dying and the Living are willing to participate in final conversations with the goal of having honest communication, then the Living often see a decrease in their stress, and everyone adjusts better to the circumstances.

No Regrets

One example that highlights the coping that can be achieved through talking is Layla's story where she and her mother *talked about how we had no regrets in our relationship. I stayed with her day and night until she passed. We both gave each other everything we had to give in life. I held her hand, stroked her head, and kissed her forehead and loved her into the next realm.* Layla is demonstrating that the words and actions made a difference in how she coped during and after the death of her mother. Kendall specified that he was able to talk with his father, while others in his family did not, and that it *helped him to come to terms with his death faster than other family members.*

Vulnerability

Charli talked about the importance of her mother being vulnerable and honest about what she was going through, which allowed her to express what she was feeling. Specifically, she stated that *I was only thirteen, so I really did not understand what it meant until I saw all the physical, emotional, and spiritual pain my mother was in. By witnessing that pain, it allowed me to express mine.* Upon reflection she realized that in the long run, being present and open to her mother's death journey helped her to express all her emotions, especially her sadness, and helped her to cope with her death. Dayla also confirmed the importance of these interactions: *I feel like if I wouldn't have had any final conversations, then coping would have been much more difficult.*

Witnessing the Dying's Peace

Jaddi told us that his *final conversations helped all our family stay positive and rational and not in hysteria, because their father was calm and at peace with his death journey.* Demariz concurred: *If I wouldn't have had the chance to speak with her, the aftermath would have been much harder for me. It gave both of us a sense of peace.* Larry found that their talks continued even after his father's death: *In one of the last conversations I had, he told me, "I have a couple books I want you to read." I went ahead and read those books. I found solace in the words he never got to tell me. I think it puts me more at peace.* We have found that there can be hidden messages from the Dying if you pay attention and follow your intuition. Larry was curious enough to go look for and read those books that his father wanted to share with him, and in them, he found peace and a way to cope with his loss.

PERSONAL GROWTH

The death of a loved one is often a difficult time when the Living are pushed past their comfort level. Confronted by challenging experiences, the Living become motivated to make sense of those experiences. That search for meaning can lead to positive changes in life and personal growth. Accompanying the Dying along their death journey can be distressing and demanding. What is surprising is that the *more* the Living engage in final conversations with the Dying, the more the Living are prepared to learn about themselves and their lives from those talks.

Relating to Others

Relating to others refers to the importance of being more open, emotionally expressive, and compassionate within relationships. Victoria revealed: *I think what I learned from watching him is how important the person who is dying is and the insight that they share with the Living. I learned that any of us might not be alive tomorrow. I try to remember to live like I'm dying, that we are all dying, that every moment is precious. That I don't want to leave anything unsaid, any lessons untaught, or freedoms unused. Part of this thing about not living out of ego. To live out of love.* Ellen learned that she needed to prioritize *what's important in life, which is sharing your love and sharing your relationship. All the other stuff is just the noise around us. I try to remember that we live in a universe where it's possible you could be here one day and not the next. I want people in my life to truly know how I feel about them. It reaffirmed that it was really very important to not withhold stuff from people in my life.*

New Possibilities

New possibilities are created when the Living are stirred to move forward, trying new things and changing life's priorities. Scott told us that his dad *felt like he never worked a day in his life. He followed his passions, and it led to happiness and success. So, I need to find my passion.* Hector also focused on an insight that his friend shared with him: *My dying friend was a testament to the fact that life should be lived positively and full-heartedly. He wanted others to celebrate his life and not to mourn, and that is what our last conversation was about. I try to live as though his spirit is here. I want to remain positive and keep him alive by talking about him with our families or mutual friends.* Hector also noted that this change in attitude didn't take away his sadness and loss of his dear friend, rather it showed him what to focus on—new possibilities.

Personal Strength

Personal strength describes the feeling of self-reliance that the Living build through their final conversations. This strength supports the Living's perception of their own competence to handle future challenges. Betty Lynn was raised in and lived in a very masculine, non-emotional world. Her undergraduate degree was in animal science, and she had a successful, 18-year career as an agricultural salesperson. Then, she participated in her first final conversation and had a very powerful experience, which resulted in her choosing to go back to graduate school to become a licensed counselor (recall Betty Lynn's spiritual experience with CJ from Chapter 8). After being a counselor for a few years, she then became a deacon in her church. She told us *that she knew that there was more that she could do, that she had to do, that she had found a "calling" and that she felt that she was destined to do more with her gifts and talents.* Once she became a licensed therapist, she talked with many more people who were close to death, as well as their family members. She explained: *At first it didn't seem dramatic, but in a lot of ways it was more dramatic, because of where I had started, in a world of men with few emotions expressed, to a world of emotions at the end of life. My journey has been reinforced because of all of my final conversations.* She explained the impact of her journey by saying, *Yeah, it's draining, it's tough, it's hard, but I'd still do it again today. You know, when someone at the church needs me, I'm there for them.*

Because of the personal growth that Betty Lynn experienced as a result of her end-of-life experiences, she discovered some new personal strengths: openness, empathy, honesty, increased spirituality, and the ability to express and receive all types of emotions. She found a new aptitude to talk with anyone about very challenging topics. She also proved to herself that she has the capacity to continually push herself, so that she can be the best that she can be. Her words of advice to others are to "*Be open to it in whatever form it may come. Don't try to limit it to what you think it should be. Do not be afraid of them." There are numerous times, daily, that I find myself saying things and have no clue where it is coming from. But because it is brilliant, I go with it. I believe I have learned to let go and let God.*

God or whatever higher power there may be. I've worked with all kinds of different faiths, including atheists, and the work has progressed very well because I accept them where they are.

Ellen's husband, Michael, died from a brain tumor. They were told that he only had a little time to live following a major surgery, but then he went on to live for six months. Their interactions over those six months showed her that she was stronger than she ever knew possible. Her personal growth came from the sum of all their interactions. She knew that her most important job was to prepare her children for a life without their father. *It was up to me to let my kids know that their life wasn't normal. We had plenty of laughs, but we don't have the same life as people around us. It became my responsibility and my job. I saw this very clearly that the kids would make their own decisions whether they grew up with a chip on their shoulder and were mad at the world, or whether they grew up more loving and compassionate. It was my job to make sure that they grew up more loving and compassionate rather than that life had screwed them—which life had. They lost their father when they were young. And kids who lose their parent young, it never goes away. It is my responsibility to make sure that they are strong.* Ellen had to become stronger than she ever knew possible to succeed in protecting and teaching her two children. Ellen went on to talk about the successful adults that her two small children had grown into two decades later.

Spiritual Change

Spiritual change implies an adjustment or enhancement of religious or spiritual beliefs. Roy, an elder in a traditional church and a very logical attorney, shared with us a story that compelled him to embrace some spiritual beliefs, even if they weren't entirely consistent with his religious foundation. He shared: *I don't understand how spiritual matters work. I'm 85 now; when I was 45, I could have given you a scholarly answer. I do not know how the spirit works. I do know the spirit is alive. I do believe in a God who is alive. And my mother did. She was personally acquainted with Him.* That last point was verified to him during their final conversation (in Chapter 8). Roy went on to explain that while he was still religious, he was now more spiritual. He was okay with not understanding how the spirit works; he cherished his new expanded spiritual beliefs.

Melissa self-described as not religious, whereas she described her grandparents as very religious. A day before her grandmother's death, she told Melissa, *I feel funny.* This message became profound for Melissa because *I think she was dying. She was spiritually between worlds at that point in time. I think that's evidence of it. I mean, "I feel funny"—it's not, "I feel sick," "I feel cold," "I feel bad," "I hurt"—she said, "I feel funny." That to me suggests that there is some sort of a transition.*

This evidence of a transition made by her grandmother would take on greater significance in the months to follow. As Melissa told us prior to her final conversations, she had questions about spiritual messages. She shared a story about her departed grandparents coming back to talk with her, with the specific goal of helping her to have faith and to push her to find her spirituality. *I was standing by this tree, and I had an experience. I don't know how to explain it in words. But I really think that my grandma and my grandpa came to me—I think specifically my grandpa did, to prove to me that there is a spiritual world. He's like, 'Melissa, there's something out here. You have to believe in it.' My grandma and grandpa were both there; it's like they won't let me ignore it. They won't let me, and it's not that I don't believe in spirituality, I just have a really hard time with Catholicism and the religious aspect of it. But that was meaningful to me, because again, I think that it was just a reassurance by them that they were there and that it exists. I need to stop—not ignoring it—but I need to figure out how to deal with this. If it's not through religion, it's through something else.* Melissa would continue to reflect on her final conversations, as well as her dreams of her grandparents interacting with her after their deaths. Her own spiritual growth emerged from these reflections over time.

Appreciation for Life

Appreciation for life means resetting priorities to focus on what is important and increasing gratitude for life. In the face of death, we often learn to appreciate life, which often dictates a need to reset priorities to focus on what is important.

Following the death of his mother, Andrew learned to prioritize his family: *I was reminded that nothing is more important than family, and grew closer to my father, siblings, and children.* Tessina also shared new priorities. *It helped me to try and live my life how he suggested—it gave me focus. His philosophy was to give everyone the benefit of the doubt, that it didn't matter what your background was; people were people.*

Derrick's father had died when he was young, and now his beloved grandfather, who had stepped into the father role for him, was dying. He shared that his final conversation *changed him from being indecisive and making bad choices, to being more decisive and using the resources and the days that are given to me to benefit my life and others around me. Since my conversations with my grandfather, I have been wiser as far as what choices I've made. I've made sure that where I am going is leading to something, and I think that I value that over anything else. I needed to make sure for the rest of my life that I did the best for all of us. I am going to carry on our name, and I am going to make us all proud.*

SUMMARY

Positive outcomes of final conversations include acceptance, closure, coping, and personal growth. Acceptance often comes from two things: the Living witnessing the physical decline and pain of their loved one, as well as hearing the Dying's own acceptance of their approaching death. It helps to hear the Dying talking openly about their personal experiences during their end-of-life journey. Closure comes from leaving nothing left unsaid, clearing the air, and having time with the Dying to share messages of love and to say a final goodbye. Coping arises from having no regrets from the time left together, being vulnerable and open with one another during the conversations, and witnessing the peace that the Dying may experience as part of their journey. Personal growth may arise from: finding new ways to relate to others, exploring new possibilities, becoming more self-reliant and acknowledging newfound personal strength, experiencing spiritual growth, and finally, gaining a new appreciation for life.

TIPS FOR BETTER CONVERSATIONS

- When you love someone so much that you think you cannot live through their death yourself, that is when you really have to make yourself participate in final conversations. To be able to say what needs to be said helps the Dying and the Living cope. These conversations help the Living begin to make the transition to their life without the Dying.
- The good goodbye is more likely if the Dying have all their needs taken care of. Sometimes this will require the help of hospice care, so both the Living and the Dying receive guidance with the end-of-life journey.
- Take care to watch, listen, and respect what the Dying are saying and doing. Denying what is going on only prevents the Dying from being able to help you gain acceptance, closure, coping, and personal growth.
- The people who benefit the most from acceptance, closure, coping, and personal growth are those who actively participate in as many interactions as possible.
- Do not go into final conversations with the expectation that you will receive any or all of these outcomes. Go into them with an open heart and with a goal of sharing precious time, messages, and memories with your loved one. Often these hidden gifts appear after the death, sometimes weeks, months, or even years later upon reflection.

chapter 11

Out of the Mouths of Babes: Children Talk About Their Final Conversations

Final conversations help a lot because you can express how you feel right then and there. It's comforting to know that you had that with them. It gives you closure and acceptance, and I also think it means a lot more when you see that the person is okay, and then you can be okay with it. It just helps you before they die. (Jayne)

CHILDREN TELL US HOW TO SAY GOODBYE

Children think about death differently than adults do. It takes some maturity to think about something you haven't experienced. And experiencing the death of a loved one makes for an unusually mature child. Jayne was 12 when her mother died, but 9 when she was diagnosed with cancer. She had the opportunity to learn about dying from her childhood into her adolescence. Jayne was one of the many children we interviewed in bereavement camps. These children had good support for their grieving process. Nevertheless, they each handled it differently.

We found that most of their last interactions were about everyday concerns, although their conversations also touched on love, self-image, and spiritual experience. We asked them what advice they would give other people going through the death of a loved one, and they were forthcoming about what they thought other kids and adults should do faced with a similar situation.

Not all children had as many opportunities for final conversations as they would have liked. Some children mentioned that they had difficulty speaking to loved ones, either because the Dying was beyond the point of speaking or because they were not allowed to have alone-time with them. For Emaline, both reasons were in play. She was nine when her grandfather was dying. Advanced cancer had robbed him of speech, so the adult caregivers restricted access to him. *He would just lay in his bed all day, and we were told not to disturb him, so we couldn't go back to his room.*

For others, the restriction had more to do with the numbers of people present during the Dying's final days and their unwillingness to accept the impending death. Peter, 13 when his uncle died of liver cancer, speaks of this problem with goodbyes. *Whenever that day came, it was like we didn't even get to say goodbye because we didn't want to. We wanted him to stay. So, no one really wanted to say goodbye to him.* This hesitancy to say goodbye is not limited to children. But it is up to the adults to accept the fact of death and help the child gain the private time with the Dying they may need and want.

We sort these last conversations of children by age level, as their stage of development affects how they understand and talk about death. When you see a parenthesis in one of the children's quotes, we are indicating that the interviewer is asking for clarification or inserting a clarifying word.

TALKING WITH THE DYING THROUGHOUT CHILDHOOD

Preschool (4–6 years old)

Children up to age six understand the world based on their own limited experience. So, if grandpa drank a lot of beer, and most especially if adults commented negatively about his drinking, a child, like five-year-old MacKenzie, might conclude that his habit killed him. When asked what disease he had, she replied: *He didn't have a disease. My grandpa died because he was sick and he drunk so much beer and that's how he got so sick. He didn't have no cancer but it's 'cause he was drinking beer.*

Some preschoolers will merely dismiss what is not in their experience, even though the adults may try to explain death and its causes. Faith at four years had been told her father was dying of cancer. *He told me one day, "I am going to die," and I was like, "Whatever," 'cause I was like four, and he said, "No, I'm serious," and I was like, "Whatever," and my mom said, "No, it's true," and like two weeks later, he got cancer. And then one day he told me, "Tomorrow, I might die, and I love you."* Clearly, for Faith the death was not very real, even though she was allowed access to her dad until his death. She observed: *The worst part was when he was dead. He looked funny.* Then she went off on several long, imaginative stories about birthday cake, pregnant monkeys, dolphins, a dog named Baby who was poisoned. Well, you get the idea. Faith had a wild imagination and did not understand the finality of death. So, it will be up to Faith's loving adults to continue this conversation into the future. She will have questions, and she will need those around her to help her understand that death is final; that she can trust that she is still protected, loved, and cared for by those around her; and that her dad truly loved her and didn't want to leave her. Continuing to share stories from when dad was still alive will bring comfort, eventual understanding, and even permission for Faith to talk about her dad.

Very young children may engage in magical thinking of the sort that leads them to believe that death can be caused by their own thoughts or feelings. Not having yet developed the ability to think realistically about the relationship between cause and effect (i.e., between illness and death), they may think that something they did or thought caused a loved one's death. Such a belief, that their "bad" thought or behavior killed a loved one, can stay with them a long time, resulting in unwarranted guilt. More on this is found later under Tips for Better Conversations.

Grammar School (7–11 years old)

Children from about seven until their teens are more capable of causal thinking. They understand that some diseases can cause death and that death is final. They understand rules—the idea that behavior has consequences—and they value the structure of knowing what those rules are so they can avoid the worst of the consequences. Therefore, they want the truth; they value openness with their family members. Because they need and want structure, they depend on the predictable routine interactions that families use to structure their lives, such as shared mealtimes, familiar games, bedtime stories, doing household chores together, and engaging in outdoor activities. They use small talk, such as reports of school events, weather, and sports to share time and their daily lives with each other.

Openness. Cleveland, at 11, felt that the best part of his final conversation with his mother was that she was honest with him and she trusted him to contribute to family life when she was gone. *It was important that she said that I was going to have to be a lot more responsible and help take care of the twins more. She got a lot more open, and I liked how she was like that because she believed that I could cope with everything.*

Family Rituals. Nita, her twin Hayley, and seven other siblings lost their father, an Air Force pilot, to cancer. Nita and her 10-year-old brother Luke each independently shared the ritual of their father acting like an airplane or having them act like an airplane. Luke recalled: *He would always pretend I was an airplane and hold me up there.* In her own interview, Nita confirmed: *My dad would act like an airplane and kind of go around, hold his wings out of the plane, and it was funny too.* The children in this large family identified with their father and his career using this ritual he created. From time to time, the children continue to use this behavior to remind them of their father.

Tweens and Teens (12–18 years old)

The teenage years, as every parent knows, are full of upheaval and change. They are a time to question the rules you learned so carefully in childhood. It is a time of trying on different roles and identities to see who you might be. It is also a time when you need some trusted adults, often *not* your parents, to try out ideas and question the rules. Sometimes, in pushing the limits of acceptable behavior, teens experience anger, resentment, and if things blow up, guilt. Then those trusted adults become necessary sounding boards. Teens experiencing the death of a loved one can step up to responsibility, or they can become resentful of their losses. One thing that seems to help is openness. A teen does not want to be lied to or kept in the dark.

Openness. Jayne was 9 when her mother was diagnosed and 12 when she died. Looking back to this transition period from her early teens, she recalls needing the truth. *I was always glad I was in the know. I didn't want it sugarcoated. If I did, I literally hit the person till they told me, which is really weird because I was 9, 10 years old, and it didn't hurt very much. I always wanted the straight truth. Even though some of the people in my extended family didn't think that was right. My dad always thought it was the right thing to do. I really appreciate that. My mom and I talked about it, and she said: "I know it's going to be hard on you, but it's okay to move on. It's okay for you to have other mother figures. She wasn't selfish with me, which I appreciated. She was just great with that. She always let me know I was really wanted and really cared about, and whatever was going on with her, she would tell me; she wouldn't say, "Oh, honey, I'm fine." If she wasn't feeling good, she would tell me.*

Love gifts. Toby's father wrote a book about his life to give to each of his nine children, along with a personalized letter and video-recorded blessing for each child with advice and direction for their lives. At his death, when Toby was 11, each child was given their personal book, letter, and recording. Toby appreciated the preparations his father made for his absence. Far from feeling abandoned, as children can feel when a parent dies, Toby knew he was cared for and cherished. About the letter with its personalized advice, he said: *I knew that it came from him and not like something he got from somewhere else. And that's what he really wanted us to do. It meant that he really cared about us, and he was preparing us for his death because he figured that he wasn't going to make it, and he was preparing all of us for it.*

ADVICE FROM KIDS TO KIDS AND FOR KIDS

We asked the children what they would tell other children to help them get through the death of a loved one. Further, we asked what they would tell the Dying about what a child needs from them. We found their responses so useful that we will share the advice with you in their words before we summarize. Most of their advice to kids was about making sure that the Dying knows the relationship continues to be important, but also included staying upbeat, and using the support they have available to cope. Their advice to the Dying was similar to the first piece of advice to children: affirm the importance of their relationship. They also advised the Dying to be open and real, and to reveal what they know about the beloved child they must leave.

Advice for Kids Facing the Death of a Loved One

Affirm Your Relationship: Spend the Time, Reveal Yourself, Show Your Love, Be There. Caelen regretted not taking opportunities to be with his father. He wants to tell others faced with these choices: *If he asked you to spend time with him, go spend time with him. Don't hesitate. Do every single thing you can with him before he leaves you.*

Rachel was 17 when her grandmother died. She wants you to just go and spend the time, so you avoid any regret. *I would say to just go and just talk to them about everything, and just take some time out of your week; I decorated her bulletin board at her nursing home for her; we just hung out; we didn't talk about anything specific except the pictures she had in her room. Just the way we talked, I mean it really had no rhyme or reason to it. It was just 'cause it was the last moments we had, so I would just say go spend some quality time and chat with them.*

Matt was 13 years old when his dad died and felt it was important that his dad knew who he was before he died. His advice: *I would hug them and tell them that they should say lots of things about themselves that their parents don't know—that way they don't have the gut feeling that they never told them what they are like.* He felt that it would be a mistake to feel forever that your dad never knew you.

Love messages were clearly important in the large family that Dan and Toby inhabited. Their father died when they were 9 and 13. Dan, the younger boy at nine, suggests nonverbal love gestures: *Every day give them twice as many hugs, twice as many kisses.* While Toby, the teenager, proposes direct verbal messages: *Well, always tell them that you love them because they are just about to die, and they want to know that their kids are thinking of them.* Each person may find their own way of expressing love, but these kids say: do it somehow. Otherwise regrets have a way of popping up later. Nine-year-old Autumn felt she was not explicit enough with her love: *I wish I said I love you before he died.* And Mia, who was 14 when her grandmother died, admitted: *I know I said I love you a lot, but I feel like I didn't say it enough, and I wish I could have said it more.*

Showing love can also include little kindnesses and keeping things light. Joshua, after his father died when he was 10, said, *Be kind. And Luke, also 10, adds: If there is anything they can do that would make their dad (the Dying) really happy, then they should do it.*

Jayne summed it up well by emphasizing that this is your time to be there and show your love; it's all unique to you. *It doesn't always have to be something that you say or you think should be said. Nothing should be forced. You shouldn't feel like you have to have a deep conversation. It's not anybody else's time. It's not time to talk about your extended future. This is your time with them and you need to take it seriously, 'cause they are not always going to be there. If you don't want to say anything, just hold their hand.*

Be Strong; Stay Positive. Some of our children had a hard time with the process and wanted to get through it well. They seemed to be truly concerned for others who might have difficulty coping with the inevitability of death too. Donny, who wanted to control his emotions when his grandmother died, was 11 at the time and must have taken it hard. He offers: *Just be prepared because everything dies. If she does die, then just let it out, but don't let it out on everyone else.* Donny, or someone he knows, must have acted out in their grief and then regretted it. Avery, 16 when her grandmother died, advises: *Just don't feel like it's your fault. And just try to move on you know because everybody dies.*

Other children just want you to move through the process smoothly and without drama. Perhaps there were family members trying to soothe them with similar words. Fiona at 13 said goodbye to her grandmother. She suggests: *Just stay calm and relax, and it will be okay.* Similarly, 10-year-old Chloe offers: *Just be strong; everything will be fine.* Although these examples may seem to be oversimplifying a difficult process, they are true attempts to soothe kids who probably struggled with the emotions raised during their final conversations.

Talk to Supportive Adults; Find Your Trusted Others. We spoke with children in bereavement camps, so they were more in touch with the idea of support systems than other children might be. As a result, they gave good advice about finding others who can help. Miranda wanted kids to know: *You have other people that love you and that know how you feel.* Autumn agrees: *Sit down and talk about it, with anybody around like friends, parents.* Megan, 17, urges: *Don't be afraid to let it out—your concerns, your thoughts, your fears.*

Most of these children seemed to know that trusted adults can provide a safe, supportive space, and some mentioned that they could also serve as emotional outlets. Samuel, who was only eight when his father died, suggests: *Talk about it to any adults you trust. And make sure that if you want to cry, don't be embarrassed about it. It just makes you feel better. It's easier to tell an adult about your feelings than try to hold them in.*

Robin has a bit of advice for the members of the child's support system: parents, extended family, teachers, therapists. She urges patience with children so they can have time to deal with their own thoughts and emotions. She suggested that children and teens should be asked questions to see where they are at in the process. Some of the questions she valued going through her grandmother's death at 17 included: *How are you feeling about this? Are you ready to go see your granny? Are you okay with spending more time with her?*

Advice for the Dying When Interacting with Kids

Affirm Your Relationship: Tell Your Story. Megan, 17 when her father died, shares how much she loved hearing stories about her dad and his life. *It's kind of funny, but I think kids really like to know their parents' life stories, that they had lives before they had them, and that's kind of something that really fascinated me. I would want to know the whole story about how he met my mom—that was one that I would ask him to tell me—and stories from childhood. I loved hearing childhood stories, and I guess it was kind of fascinating to me in a way, knowing his life before I was in it. I guess it kind of made me feel more of a connection—that he's not just dad; he's a friend, a brother, a son.* If you are blessed to have time with children before your time is up, Megan would want to know you shared of yourself so they could live out their lives knowing more of the full person you were.

Be Truthful and Honest; Be Real. Fourteen when her grandmother died, Mia feels that the Dying should tell the truth about what is happening with them. *I mean being there at that moment, maybe it was overwhelming, but you have to really explain to them what's going on and maybe let the person who's dying explain because that way they're more prepared for it.* Mia implies that the more a child knows about what the Dying faces, the more prepared the child is to handle with grace the talks they want to have.

Jayne was fortunate from the ages of 9 to 12 to have loving, nurturing, and open communication with her dying mother who always kept her informed about the death process: *Keep kids in the know. There's nothing worse than telling them the full story after they die. It also depends on the kid, but I strongly believe the more you tell them, the more it's not going to hurt so bad. If you tell them a couple years later, they are going to say I wish you had told me then; I would have known more and done more. We deserve to know. Don't sugarcoat things.*

In Skylar's view, the Dying should initiate this truth-telling; they should be the first to ask the child if they have any questions: *So, I think the parent or whoever it is should ask first: Do you have questions and, if not, present the information so that they can get it later and tell them it's okay to ask. I think he should act almost the way he was before, because I think it's weird when they start acting differently. It kinda makes you feel awkward. Keep laughing and have a sense of humor with what they say and sometimes give advice. Future-wise, stay in school; don't do drugs; you know, something like around those lines; you know, keepin' it real.* Even though Skylar thought the Dying should be honest and real, she also took some of the responsibility herself. She was dedicated to staying connected with her father, even when he couldn't speak near the end of his life. And she kept the humor in their relationship. She came up with a system whereby he could tell her what he wanted with his eyes. For example, if he had an itch, he was to raise his eyebrows when she got to the right place. And they found the humor in it. *He started laughing. We both thought it was funny. I was like, I came up with something funny!*

Show What You Know About Them. One of the consequences of final conversations we found commonly among the adults was that they can have lasting effects on how the Living see themselves. For the child, these effects can be profound. Children are still actively forming an identity and feelings of self-worth. Leno was just 12, that in-between age, when his dying brother told him: *He said I was the most fun brother that he ever had.* Leno won't soon forget that he can be comforting and fun for others.

Megan knows how important it is to be approved of by a loved one, especially if you are to lose them soon, as she lost her dad when she was 17. *I would hope that any parent would tell their kids how proud they are of them, 'cause I don't think they know how much it means and how much they mean to them.*

Remember Toby who explained what his father's book and letter meant to him? His brother Matt appreciated that gift because it had advice in it that was personalized to each of his children's strengths. He clearly let each child know that he recognized who they were and what they were capable of. Thirteen when his dad died, Matt believes it is important for the Dying one *to give them advice for after they are gone.* At thirteen, self-perception may change with the day or hour. But a parent's written perspective on his child's value, ethics, and talents will help to stabilize that identity for the long term.

By speaking with their Dying loved ones, these young people learned about their talents, strengths, weaknesses, and abilities. Jayne's mother told her that although life can toss big challenges at you, it's how you handle those challenges that makes for strong identity and positive self-esteem. *I really think it's good that kids can talk to their parents, and I just hope that everybody is able to deal with it in their own way. It's not fun. It requires growing up faster than you should. And dealing with things you shouldn't at a young age. But that's life. My mom used to say you can't really control what's thrown at you, but you can control how you deal with it.* Jayne's mom made sure she knew that she was dealing with her mother's death in the best possible way, and that her mother felt Jayne was a wonderful person: *You need to be shared with the world. She really cared about me.* Jayne felt treasured. And she was.

SUMMARY

Very young children do not understand the finality of death and may create fanciful scenarios to make sense for themselves of what is happening to their loved one. School-age children are beginning to understand death and its causes. Theirs is a life based on regular, predictable routines and trust that their loved ones will be there when they need them. They are old enough to know that nothing they can do will alter the outcome, but may feel some misplaced responsibility for the death. Children remember final conversations that are honest and open, that continue everyday routines, and that reveal how loved they are by the Dying. These talks maintain their relationship with the beloved up to and beyond death.

Teenagers are learning to question the rules, question authority, and find new authorities. They remember good final conversations as truthful and real. They often recall their loved one as understanding and forgiving of their mistakes, and generous with loving gestures and approval. When they begin to realize the benefits of the talks, they realize that the time spent is worthwhile and they are maturing as a result. In the next chapter, we will hear from adults who had final conversations when they were children and how they feel they were changed by them over time.

TIPS FOR BETTER CONVERSATIONS

The children were very forthcoming with their advice. To kids: affirm the relationship by being there and showing your love, be positive, and find your support. To the Dying: affirm the relationship by telling your story, be truthful and real, and reveal what you know about the child you must leave. We have a few suggestions too, for parents and other relatives and friends of a child who may need assistance in starting and processing their last words with a Dying loved one.

- Very young children do not understand the finality of death. And they may be fanciful in their attempts to understand it. Allow them their own views, but be ready when they have questions later in their development.

- Use appropriate language according to their age; speak clearly, plainly, and simply. Avoid the use of euphemisms for death and dying such as "sleeping, passed away, earned his wings," etc., so that you don't confuse the child.
- Make sure children have access to their loved one if they want it. Approach the child with explanations about what is happening and then ask questions to find out what the child needs (e.g., "Would you like to have some one-on-one time with your dad? If yes, when do you want to talk with him?"). Follow through with their desires about contact if you are able.
- Don't force children and/or teens to talk with the Dying. Ask them what their concerns and fears are about interacting with the Dying (e.g., "Are you afraid you'll say something wrong?"). Then gently allay their fears and encourage them to give it a try.

chapter 12

Growing Up

I think through final conversations you can talk to them about stuff and begin to deal with it at your own pace, and that is really a good thing. It's not something anyone wants to happen to them. It's not something I would wish upon someone, but it does make you grow up, understand things at an earlier age, and it does put things into perspective. (Jayne)

Talking with someone who is dying changes you. It changes the way you view your own mortality, and it changes your trust in the stability of relationships. It can change the way you view yourself in the world. Now that you know what children say about their final conversations, we will look at the memories that linger for adults who had them in childhood and how it made them grow up more quickly than they may have done otherwise. Their final conversations led to further growth as they reflected on them years later as adults.

LOOKING BACK TO THE EFFECTS OF CHILDHOOD GOODBYES: GETTING REAL

Children don't know much about death; they gradually get clues about it and begin to consider it more seriously at puberty. When we're young, most of us don't have to consider how death will affect us. But some do. In today's ocean of electronic media, young children flounder with the task of separating the real from the make-believe, particularly when faced with media images of violence and death.

Children who live with a dying relative every day learn about that reality early in life.

Say What You Feel

Jeanette was 18 when she recalled for us the death of her grandfather, Weber. He was much more than a typical grandfather to her. After her father left, the family expanded to include her maternal grandparents. On the face of it, the new living situation was so Jeanette's mother could help care for her own mother, who had multiple sclerosis. But the fortunate side effect was that Grandfather Weber became the father figure that she and her sister needed. *My grandfather spent half the time with us and the other half in his house in L.A. And then every summer I'd go to L.A. with him. So, we were very close.* On the brink of puberty, Jeanette began to realize how special her grandfather was to her. And that it was up to her to let him know. *He was very quiet and sort of stoic. He said that he loved you, but he didn't elaborate. I think it was the first time that I got to tell him how much he meant to me. I mean he knew, but I really wanted him to know just how much he'd done for me.* As a teenager looking back, Jeanette is grateful for that opportunity to say what she felt, because she already recognized that *you hide feelings from yourself.*

One distinctly personal effect Jeanette noted from this experience was the insecurity it produced in her. *I know that it made me look at my grandmother, who had been getting even worse, and I started thinking, "What have I told her?" And then, my mother and my sister. Especially since it happened so suddenly—I hadn't known at all that he was sick—I started thinking: What's going to happen to everyone else that I love?*

Each child will react somewhat differently to the death of a loved one, depending on their age, their relationship to the Dying, and the experience they are allowed to have of the death. For some, the death of someone so close may produce insecurity and guilt. But children who have time with the Dying and who receive affirmations of love from them can gain new appreciation for the relationship they had and for the self they are becoming.

It's Not Your Fault

Ruth's father died when she was five. Now an adult, she recalls his care for her as he died of cancer. What is critical to a very young child is the bond of trust they have with parents. Ruth's father, Kerry, seemed to know intuitively that to die without explaining his leaving could destroy this trust. It could leave Ruth's ability to form later relationships greatly damaged. Here she recalls the last time she spoke with him. *He essentially just said to me that he wanted to die. Not because he wanted to leave us or anything. I just remember him being really, really, really, really happy to be alive, and really, really not all that upset to be dying, just like it was the next natural step. I remember at the very end he would say things like: "I want to die. I don't want to leave you. I'm not scared. You don't need to be scared; everything's natural." It was like he was trying to free me of being angry at God. And I don't know why I didn't get angry at him. To me, I would think, "Oh, you want to die. You bastard." But I didn't, I was just like, "Okay, that's the way it's supposed to be. Sure." And that was just totally natural—him telling me he was going to die. I don't remember being told he had cancer; I don't remember knowing it was coming; it was just like every day had been the way Dad had said it was supposed to be. And this was the next thing Daddy said was supposed to happen.* Ruth trusted her father to know how the world worked. Her father was at peace with his life and his death. When a young child loses a parent, there will be inevitable repercussions in later life, whether it is guilt that they were responsible, distrust of enduring relationships, or confusion about how to be what the absent parent expected. As Ruth says: *Everything changes when your father dies when you're five.* The best that the Dying can do is speak and act with love until their end and assure that the child will be surrounded by love and support from the remaining caregivers after the Dying is gone.

You Have a Right to Feel Resentful

Dana also lost her father, but a little later in her life. He was first diagnosed with a brain tumor when Dana was 8, and finally lost his battle when she was 12. She had quite a lot of time to prepare for his death. Eventually her father's disease worsened to the point where he couldn't talk but could still interact. She visited him regularly in the hospital, and as she relates, these unusual interactions became the norm for her. She recalls feeling duty bound and experiencing some resentment about missing out on childhood's usual freedoms.

The information revolved around I love you. I always thanked him for how much he taught me. I always told him that I would never forget him. That I would always remember him. And after doing it every Sunday and usually a night during the week and sometimes on Saturdays, it became really rote. Especially for an 11-year-old, when you have to learn something and you do it again and again, it's like a script. I remember many times, being 11 and thinking, (sigh), this could be the last time I'm talking with my dad, and I sound like a script. Because I knew what a script was. You know, I'd been in plays and memorized my lines to the Dancing Pumpkin, and that's not how I wanted it to be. My capacity for word choice was limited, and I didn't know exactly what I wanted to say. And then there were times where I was like, okay, if I could just say goodbye to my dad now, I get to go home and meet my friends for ice cream later. There were some feelings of resentment because I was missing out on some of my socialization with my friends.

Dana's feelings of missing out on things that other 12-year-olds were doing is fairly common for a child who is losing a parent. Such loss involves the child emotionally, and in doing so, interrupts her young life. It may be difficult for children to admit—or effectively deal with—the frustration that they can experience during a long journey toward death. Fortunately, Dana's mother, Ellen, had asked counselors about the best way to prepare her children for their father's death. Today, as an adult, Dana can acknowledge her childhood frustrations with parts of her final conversations, yet she is grateful that her mother encouraged her to participate in them.

Have No Regrets

Dana is left with healthy feelings about herself, her father, and about death. *Not to be morbid, but when each day is going to be our last, I mean you always hear people say, "Well, you don't know when you're going to die. You could get hit by a truck." Yeah, knock on wood, we're not getting hit by trucks, but you don't know. Because life is so uncertain, and it's so precious simultaneously, I had the chance to say goodbye to my father. I said a really, really,* ***good goodbye.***

Dana not only had the support of her parents, but she also benefited from professional counseling as well. She was prepared to have no regrets about her goodbyes to her father.

I always felt like that final conversation could be my last. And so I need to take it. And I didn't want to feel guilty or upset, I didn't want any should'ves. At 12 that was very important. I didn't want should've. I don't want should've when I'm 50 or 60 or 70.

TEENS' FINAL CONVERSATIONS: A CRASH COURSE IN ADULTHOOD

Teenagers are typically ego centered. And that's a good thing. They are finding out who they are, what they think, how they feel, and what they want to do about it. But teens faced with the death of a dear one are challenged to consider someone else before themselves. Unlike young children, teens have considered the meaning of death and mortality. If they do rise to the occasion and wish to interact with their loved one, they can feel resentful about the time and effort it takes to engage. If they don't, they can feel guilty. Either way, it's stressful and life changing. It can propel teens into maturity before their time.

You'll Grow Up Fast

Over 20 years following her father's death, Karen clearly remembered her final conversations with her father from when she was a teen. *I do remember my father saying that he loved us and how proud he was of us.*

Karen admits that losing a father when she did interrupted her adolescence and propelled her toward premature adulthood. And that experience gave her a perspective different from her peers'. *I grew up really, really fast. You know, I went from a 15-year-old girl to a 25-year- old woman in a week. It was just at the end of my freshman year of high school. I can remember sitting at football games and stuff, and looking at the cheerleader girls going, "Daddy, Daddy, take my picture." And I'm thinking: You just don't know; you just don't know what you have.*

I was just in such a different place from everybody else, emotionally and spiritually, having gone through this experience. It was a crash course in adulthood, really.

Following her father's death, Karen became a bit wild during her teen years and was thankful that she didn't suffer any negative consequences from her rebellious acts. She believes that it was the death that propelled her into her wild actions. But it was the last interactions that helped her eventually find peace. As Karen put it, *A final conversation is not a prophylactic for reactive behavior, but it can offer some comfort in the moment and upon reflection in the years that follow.* Her father's legacy of love sustained Karen through her abbreviated adolescence and propelled her toward feeling older, wiser, but perhaps a bit cheated of her teen years.

Feel Empathy If You Can, but Forgive Yourself If You Can't

Claire was 17 when her uncle Matthew died of AIDS. She vividly recalls being a typical self-involved teenager. And, as clearly, she remembers her uncle's forgiveness and wisdom. Matthew had been an energetic psychiatric nurse before the disease began to incapacitate him. He had wanted to make a special event of Claire's completion of a bike ride for charity. But it wasn't meant to be.

When we came across the finish line, he was there, along with our parents, and that was a happy time. But I remember focusing on him. For the first time, I had seen him not being positive. He really was in pain. I remember he lay down on this little bench, and he was complaining, "Oh, I'm in so much pain." And it was horrible, 'cause my mom and I were both frustrated. We didn't know how to respond to it. Anger was the first thing that came out instead of sympathy. Here it was a happy time, but instead it was like, "You should be in bed; you need to be resting." And it wasn't the right reaction at all. I remember he wanted to do everything perfectly. He got a room at the Hyatt Regency downtown and wanted us all to spend the night. We went to the hotel and he was upstairs. I didn't even go up there, but my mom had gone up to speak to him. I will always regret that I never went up there to talk to him.

Claire's uncle had some insight into the mindset of a teenager and made sure he spoke with her about the botched party. Undoubtedly his background in psychology helped him to understand, but it was his affection for his niece that led him to forgive her for the failed celebration. *Instead of me bringing it up and saying, "Oh, Uncle Matt, you know, I'm so sorry about this," he was the one who brought it up. He was very strong about it. He wasn't tiptoeing around the subject; he just said, "You know, I don't know what happened back there, but I don't want you to have any guilt. I'm going to be gone, and you're going to have to go on. So, I just want to tell you whatever happens, you remember, I don't want you to have any guilt." He was beyond understanding: "Well, you know, you're young and I understand." After that, I told him "I am just so sorry, I'm sorry." And he said, "I don't want to hear that. I forgive you. It's okay."* Claire remembers still her uncle Matthew's message: *"Don't feel guilty about feeling good."*

Teenagers may be self-involved, but they are also immersed in a time of great personal change and sensitivity to the uniqueness of others. Indeed, the death of a loved one can compel them to look at the world from the Dying's viewpoint. They may have regrets about what they did or did not do during the dying process. But they will remember the needs of the Dying that they were able to meet, and they will remember their own needs that were met by the Dying. And they will come to see themselves as different from their carefree peers, but grateful for the chance to participate in the Dying's end time.

YOUNG ADULTS' FINAL CONVERSATIONS: CHALLENGES IN CHANGING TIMES

Perhaps the busiest and most challenging time of life, young adulthood is a time of action, reflection, and change. Typically, as teens graduate from high school, they move on to higher education, training, or a job. No matter what path is taken, the challenge is mastery—of skills, of concepts, of a body of knowledge. With mastery comes accomplishment, and with accomplishment comes responsibility. And with responsibility comes reflection on how to make good decisions. Young adults are challenged to figure out what they will stand for. They are building character. And they can be merciless perfectionists. This makes having final conversations—something they most likely have never practiced or studied—a daunting prospect. But those who do it anyway may discover that being perfect isn't as important as being human.

Embrace Your Imperfection

Tory was 21 when her 19-year-old brother, Jacob, died. The diagnosis of leukemia had been a long time coming after months of symptoms. The leukemia was in remission when he suffered a brain hemorrhage from the effects of chemotherapy. Even though he was the younger sibling, Tory looked up to her brother as smart, generous, and forgiving. She spent as much time as she could with him in his last months, including hours talking together on her bed. What you need to know about Tory is that she took great pride in her bed; she had the perfect pillows and quilt, and it was always perfectly made. Until they began the long talks, during which she promised to care for her brother's young son. Then they often had their conversations on her bed, so she learned to let it be messy. Tory, the perfectionist became Tory, the nurturer. She discovered several things about herself: *That I'm not as cold-hearted as I may seem. That I'm a good listener. I think that he would be proud to know that I try so hard to take care of his child. I think he would be glad to know that he picked a good person to be his godparent. I try to talk to his son about him. I think he felt better that if something happened to him, things wouldn't be that chaotic.*

Don't Wait; Say It Now

Imogene was 76 when her 25-year-old granddaughter, Breanna, said goodbye to her. Breanna was a favorite of her doting Nana, so she did her best to care for her during her decline. She speaks here about her relationship with Imogene: *I think in a way it cemented what I thought—how special we were and had that bond with each other. It's a huge family. There's like 15 grandchildren. It was special to me to know that I was special to her out of all of those. I felt some guilt because she did so much for me. I feel like I should've taken care of her more. I mean physically be there, take care of her. I had problems with my parents when I was in high school, and I lived with her for a while; she bought me a car and took care of me. I wouldn't have finished high school if it wasn't for her. She believed in me when nobody else did. And my mom—I think that my mom knew that I was feeling that way because she said, "Tell her whatever you want to tell her, because it's okay and she'll understand."*

But there were so many things I really wanted to say. Then I felt self-conscious because there were other people in the room. It was like I never got a chance, but things would go through my mind that I wouldn't say. And I kept thinking, "Why didn't I say that?" And then I'd think, "Well, the next day, when she wakes up, I'll say it."

Breanna admits that she kept putting off what she really felt was right to present a particular impression. Young adults are quite concerned with their place in the community and how they fit. Usually, they find their unique voice later in life. But Breanna recognized the difficulty of breaking out of her passive response at this critical time. *I think I saw myself as being a little bit timid because I wouldn't assert myself to say what I wanted to say, or even want to take my place beside her when somebody else was there. Feeling like maybe I'm not so important and I need to leave the room so that somebody else can be with her. But inside I was thinking, "I want to be right with her the whole time. I don't wanna leave."*

New adults are often hard on themselves for their lack of "perfection." This response is understandable, given how important it is to them to see themselves positively in relationship to the Dying, and indeed to anyone. The Living young adults felt that they more clearly saw themselves through the eyes of their loved ones and felt shifts in their self-concept.

MATURE ADULTS: GETTING REAL (AGAIN) AND SO IMPERFECT

Adulthood covers a range of ages and changes, but most of the mature adults we spoke with were middle-aged and spoke with a dying child, sibling, spouse, or parent. These adults know who they are; they have faced many of life's challenges already. But they may not have faced the loss of one so dear to them. And what they found was that the process forced them to not only shift their view of the relationship, but to also shift their view of who they are, and how they want to spend the rest of their days.

You Won't Always Be in Control

Near the end of young Jacob's time, he was affected by seizures. This last bad sign destroyed his mother Gloria's composure. *"What's wrong?" His hand started shaking, and he started laughing. And then he went into a seizure. I'm one of those people that has to be in control. I have to be on top of things. I lost it. Rebecca (Gloria's second daughter) was four months pregnant, and she was sitting there holding his hand and she goes, "Mom, snap out of it." And I ran out into the street and I screamed. And I knew what to do because my little daughter is developmentally disabled and had seizures. I knew what to do. But I couldn't do it. And I just cried and I was mad. I hated myself for being so not in control.*

I had to sit there and watch my son die. And there was nothing I could do. I couldn't take care of the "owie" this time, like I used to. Gloria gives voice to every mother's worst fear: that her child will be taken from her. As a dear friend of Julie's said after her son's death: "No mother should have to bury her child." Gloria agrees. *I don't wish for anyone to understand the loss of a child. It is tremendous. I lost my dad when I was 21, but to lose my boy is far worse.*

I'm definitely a stronger person, but weak at the same time. Imperfect, a great deal of imperfect. I cannot be in control of everything. I can't cure everything. All I can do is try to do the best I can. Gloria hung on to her strength and her opinions, but she let go of her need to feel in control. Her son led her to fearless expression of her truth.

Clean Up the Relationship

Susan's relationship with her mother, Molly, like many mother-daughter relationships, was rocky at times. Although Molly had been judgmental throughout her life, Susan's mother had criticized her throughout her life and continued to do so at the end of life. Susan began by describing a turning point with her mother, during their final conversations.

I was not built like her at all, and she always complained about my shape. I was rounder than she was. I had rounder hips, and she had no bottom at all. In those 10 days that I was there to be with her, she took five different shots at me about how big my bottom was. Finally, one day I looked at her and I said, "Mom, I'm 49 years old. I'm a grandmother. I wear a size 6. How big could I possibly be? Do you think we could give this a rest?" And she looked at me, and she never took another one of those shots again. I have to think that maybe by standing up to her, I wasn't quite who she thought I was. For the first time ever in my life, I was speaking for myself.

The new ability to defend herself led her mother to finally see Susan as an adult. Susan discovered her own voice, which resulted in a shift in Molly's perspective of her. That changed their relationship enough to allow the two of them to truly communicate in the end. Those conversations encouraged Susan to own her beauty and convictions, to be confident in who she had become, and to nurture her mother through her final days.

One of the last interactions between Susan and her mother concerned Molly's admission that she had wronged Susan. Molly's apology went a long way toward telling Susan that she mattered to her mother. *My father died when I was four, and that was another one of the things that we talked about during those dying times. She said to me that she was sorry that she had not taken me to the funeral because she thought now that it would've helped me to grieve him. That was very meaningful to me, because I was never encouraged to remember him or to grieve him; for her to say that really meant a lot. It was almost an apology. I mean it was an apology because she said, "I'm sorry I didn't." And my mother almost never apologized. So, that was very big. It was like, "How you feel matters to me, and that I did you a disservice is something that I regret."*

I always felt that I was a disappointment to her until those last few years, when I was the one that showed up. And she really did appreciate me; it helped to make up for all those years when I felt like I was not good enough.

Although it may seem to younger people that mature adults have no more growing to do, we older adults know that the habits of a lifetime of less-than-perfect relationships can weigh heavily and that we never stop growing. The mature Living partners found that in final conversations they could let go of trying to control everything, heal challenging relationships, forgive old insults, be the caregiver, and receive the gifts of feeling their own strength and confirming their adult status.

SUMMARY

The way children handle death depends greatly on the responses of the living caregivers around them. If the child is not allowed to see the Dying, there is a risk of lasting damage. The child who loses a loved one suddenly and with no explanation is likely to believe that it is their fault that the Dying abandoned them. On the other hand, the child who does speak with a dying loved one begins to understand that nothing they can do will alter the outcome. They are given the chance to express their feelings and to hear how the Dying feels about them. Children facing the death of a loved one can feel resentment about the shifts in their lives, and later, guilt about not living up to what they perceived as the standard set by the deceased. But they are also more likely to feel closure and love that stays with them for the rest of their lives.

Teenagers are growing up physically, while their emotional maturity often lags behind. They are learning about the viewpoints of others but are still wrapped up in their own perspectives. For teens, the risk of losing a loved one to death is the risk of losing a critical adult role model during a stressful time. Their challenge is to empathize, but to also forgive themselves for being self-focused.

Young adults, in their attempts to attain adult mastery in so many areas, will face the need to accept that they can say what they want to say to the Dying without needing to be "perfect."

Mature adults often think they are done with development; they are who they are, but those who participated found that these talks change them. In some cases, it is change from child to parent, as in the case of a Living child who nurtures a dying mother or father at the end of life. For others it is a process of clearing up the relationship and of relinquishing control. Indeed, it often changes what the Living choose to do with their remaining years, as we will see in the next chapter.

TIPS FOR BETTER CONVERSATIONS

Based on the Livings' experiences of growth and development, we can make a few suggestions for those of you who are interested in noting the effects of final conversations on either yourself, a child, or a teen close to you who may need assistance in processing their own last communication with the Dying.

For the Living interested in their own growth:

- Write down what you are able to as soon as possible after your final conversations. Include as much as you can of what the Dying said to you.
- When you have moved through much of your grief, go back to your journal and look at your notes with fresh eyes. What did the Dying reveal to you about you? How are you a different person today than you were then?

For all those adults who are shepherding young people through the process of coping with a dying loved one:

- Give them opportunities to speak and simply be with the Dying. They will not forget it.
- Tell them directly that it's not their fault that their loved one is leaving them. Have discussions of death and its inevitability that are simple and direct.
- Help the child avoid interpreting the loved one's death as abandonment. Leaving gifts, bequests, letters, and the like supports the belief that they were not abandoned; rather they were treasured by the Dying.
- Children experiencing the death of a loved one may have to be told directly that it is not their fault. Invite questions about the cause and reassure them about the continuing health of the other members of their family network.

- Children should also be encouraged to express their feelings about the Dying and about the death. Some of these may be expressions of love, but there also may be feelings of resentment and anger that could be received by another loving adult. This does not have to be the Dying but could be a parent or counselor. They need someone who can accept their feelings, even if they are negative outbursts. Try to remember that the anger isn't about you, but about their pain and grief.
- Some teens may feel burdened or resentful for having to take on more responsibility following the death. Try asking them how they would most like to help rather than telling them what to do. See if there are other family members or friends who can take on some of the roles and responsibilities left by the Dying so teens can still participate in the peer activities that are important for their health and maturation.
- Professional counseling is a good option for very young or very sensitive children, and necessary for the child or teen who is depressed or acting out.
- Keep the Dying alive long after their death by talking with your children about them, sharing stories, sharing laughter. If you don't talk about them, they may think that they shouldn't talk about them.

chapter 13

Going On

My friend would give me wisdom he had learned through experiencing his life fading away. He would often remind me to live my life with no regrets, to do what made me happy, to go on! (Kevin)

As we've seen, final conversations influence the ongoing development of the Living, often through changes in the maturity of their attitudes and values. But they may also change their life path.

LESSONS LEARNED: NEW WAYS OF BEING

"More Life!" Joy, Energy, Spirit

Recognizing one's own mortality leaves the Living firmly in the present moment. They don't want to waste a minute. Judy explains it this way: *After this experience, we'll go hiking on a nice day, or if someone calls me up and says, "I haven't seen you in forever," I'll say, "Let's get together now. I'm free this afternoon. What are you doing?"* Judy's joy and appreciation for life after her last interactions with her grandfather are contagious and enviable.

Others of the Living took a more philosophical view of this personal shift in their value systems. For Derrick the gift of "more life" was an energetic one. He understood his change to be the result of the energy his grandfather left behind. *I think that every action has a reaction, and I think that my reaction to his dying was more life. You know what I mean, more energy. It has to go somewhere. I didn't think about this logically; I am just thinking in retrospect. The energy lying there in the bed—this life form, his spirit—is not dying; his soul is not dying. He is around. He's gone to where souls go. But the actual form of energy that is physical was dying. Well, it has to go somewhere, and if I can claim it and take it on—psychologically or physically or physiologically or whatnot—if I can take that away and do something with it, then why not?*

Final conversations seem to help the Living learn about life and death in a very positive way. And this often involves a shift in spirituality. Roxanne's changes since her father's death have been largely spiritual. *It's made me a whole lot less judgmental. My actions, a whole lot more compassionate. I'm much more open because I've experienced something that was really not rational. I think it's made me much more spiritual and much more open. I don't know if that's reflected in how I deal with others, but it's reflected in what I do and my goals and what I choose to read, and my music, and from inside out, I think, I'm still unfolding from that.* Joy, energy, spirit—the Living find so much more life when they have taken the time and effort to speak with the Dying.

Slow Down and Take the Time

There probably are no people on earth who complain as much as Americans do about having "no time"! Who hasn't felt restricted in what they can do because of time demands from a wide variety of obligations? How many people have felt resentment about those demands? And that includes the time it takes to be with the Dying who may be approaching their deaths at the most inconvenient times for the Living. Blanca was the one to bring attention to something we probably assumed—that it takes time to have these conversations.

Blanca reminds us to take time, but also admits that she was very fortunate to be able to do so because she had a compassionate and understanding boss, as well as fortunate work circumstances. She shared that *taking the time to be with people in these times is crucial. It's more important than anything else. I'm lucky because as a therapist, I work for a therapist. My boss is just a genuinely wonderful and wise human being. And I would come to his office and say, "I've got to go to the hospital." He'd say, "Go. Take as much time as you need. These times are important and you need to spend time." He told me, "You will never regret spending a lot of time. You will regret it if you don't." He's completely right, and I'm so grateful for having a work environment that had that privilege. Because that is a privilege. Not everybody has that. I wasn't fired. I didn't lose money. I was given the space, and people covered my slack without retaliation. So that's the most important thing: I got to be with him.*

We heard this echo about the importance of time throughout the interviews, but sometimes the realization about time came too late. Jim found himself sad and depressed following his father's death. He regrets what he describes as his selfishness regarding his father. I think many children feel this way after a parent's death—that they expected to get more than they gave in that relationship. And of course, we do. That's what parent-child relationships have been about for so long. *I'm thinking, "What am I going to get out of this relationship? What's he gonna give me next?" Stuff like that, rather than thinking, "Oh, my God, I want more time with him." I want more time. I hadn't thought that before. I thought, you get together two or three days at a time, twice a year. That's fine. Talk on the phone once a month. Father's Day, Christmas gifts, birthday gifts, and that was good. I didn't want more than that. Suddenly, I wanted a lot more.* Unfortunately, we often fail to see that it's our time to give back until it's too late. Jim's new awareness spurs him to feel more intensely. *I've managed to change direction since he died. I value my mother more, my brother more. I got more sensitive and more in touch with my feelings—to others' too, but mostly to my own.* Jim cannot have any more time with his father, but he can make that time now for other loved ones.

Stop "Walking on Eggshells"

The Living often approach the Dying with fears that they may overstep their bounds, they may offend the Dying, or they may talk about things that will cause discomfort. But they eventually realize that "walking on eggshells" is just using up the precious time they have left without making the real connection they crave.

Sam was trying to figure out how to help his mother have a good death. They had a lot of talks during the last year of her life. He realized that he and his mother could both be alone in their thoughts and fears about her death, or they could take the journey together.

What I remember the most about my mom's illness when we found out that she was terminally ill with ovarian cancer was that she really would have gone through that whole process, I believe, in silence if we had let her do that. She really couldn't talk to my dad about what it was like to be dying, to be facing her own death, because it was just too painful for him.

After six months of conversation focusing on chemotherapy and other "safe" topics, Sam finally decided to be bold one day and to simply ask her a question about dying to see if she might want to talk about her death journey. *"Are you afraid of dying?" And that was really all it took for her to kind of open up. I gave her permission to talk about how she felt. It really made me realize that people who are facing their own death certainly aren't thinking about anything else during the day. So many times, people kind of walk on eggshells around them, and you don't want to bring it up. It's like the gigantic elephant in the room that nobody talks about. I think that most really want to talk about it. So, by asking her questions like how she felt, she could reveal how she was feeling. She would cry and I would cry.* As Sam points out, there is nothing wrong with crying; in fact, at times it may be the only way to let out some of the pain and fear. Finally, being able to talk about what is really in the hearts and minds of the Living and Dying is freeing. Being emotionally cautious is exhausting, and once people realize that life doesn't have to be that way, they usually experience a tremendous feeling of relief. Walking on eggshells in a relationship—any relationship—is not healthy. Censoring what you talk about in a relationship prevents you from revealing your true thoughts and feelings, as well as restricting the relationship. Specifically, at the end of life, people often avoid revealing their fears and concerns so that they don't add to the Dying's burden, but now is the time to stop walking on eggshells and be honest. Break the rules and see how freeing it can be.

Break the Rules!

Jo's father was a highly controlling person who ruled every aspect of his wife's life. He had rules not only for Mary but for his children too, including Jo. Jo knew that her mother was dying, although her father refused to accept her condition and insisted on tests and more tests. *I went down to see her. I had seen her a few times during that year. Jo's father was saying that he was about to schedule a bunch more tests for her because he was certain there was some specific thing wrong, that they could find out what it was, and that they could cure her, and she would be fine.*

He was telling us about the tests that they were going to do. I said, "Well, what does she want?" And he said, "Well, that doesn't matter." I said, "Well, yeah, it does. I just think it matters at this point what she wants and she should get to say it." He said, "No." I said, "Why?" And he said, "She's not in her right mind. She hallucinates and she doesn't understand." I said, "You know, Dad, I've never seen her hallucinate, and I've never seen her not in her right mind. I think it's strange that it never happens when I'm around." He tried to forbid me to talk to her. He said, "I don't want you to talk to her anymore." He tried to physically stop me. Because it was not allowed; I had never talked to her.

So, I went over, and I got up on the bed, and I got kinda close to her on her bed because she couldn't see very well. She had macular degeneration in one eye and shingles in the other.

I said, "You know, we're having this conversation. Dad wants you to have more tests. He feels he's going to find out what's wrong and cure you. And I feel like you should be left alone and you should be able to die in peace and not have to be pulled out and be given a test every day."

I said, "But the real important thing's what do you want? What do you want, Mom?" And she said, "I don't want any more doctors. I don't want any more tests. It's over." Then she fell back on her pillows and looked over at him and went, "I got you good."

It was astonishing to me; I've never broken the rule before. This was frightening. And she broke it too. There was nothing he could do. She died 10 days later. She died very early in the morning of the day that he had scheduled tests.

Jo had believed, from her experiences with her father, that *if I broke these rules I would die. And because I broke them, and I didn't die, I would say now, next time don't wait so long.* Given the abuse that both Mary and Jo received, their triumph together not only provided the connection Jo longed for before Mary's death but released her from the tyranny of arbitrary family rules.

Once you decide to find the time and break the rules, what will you do with that open space? Find your feelings.

Know Your Feelings, Then Voice Them

Especially when feelings are intense and tender, we often hide them from ourselves, particularly when the object of those affections may leave. As the Living will tell you, though, it's much easier and more fulfilling to feel the immensity of that love with the one who needs to know it than it is to feel it all alone when they are gone.

As we know, the last conversations aren't always sweet and positive. Sometimes you have to say the hard things as well. And it's still worth it, as Blanca tells it. *You can't keep having crap between you and expect to take care of it later. When you have those explosions, those explosions are opportunities. They're difficult. Conflict is difficult, so we avoid it. I cried my eyes out in some of those conversations. Working that conflict out with Daddy allowed for me to have a beautiful connection and peace at his death.*

Blanca found a way to face the conflict and use it. *Opportunities arise all the time for conflict resolution. It doesn't mean that you always get to do it. You have to have two parties working towards it. 'Cause he didn't like to not have the final word, but I worked with that. He wanted to have the final word. So, I'd throw in something else so we couldn't end the conversation. I knew exactly what I was doing. And Daddy loved me enough to not hang up on me. And that's a gift too, because not everybody is capable. So, it was Daddy's strength too. It was my persistence and his strength.* Blanca's wisdom is in realizing that she could not plan for the perfect resolution; she had to go through the muck of conflict with her father and allow him his say. But because she could let go of trying to control the "crap" between them, she feels peace about their relationship now.

Release Control: Let It Unfold

People want to do well. In fact, most people would prefer to do things perfectly. But what is a perfect death? And what is a perfect goodbye? We'd love to give you 10 easy steps to have the perfect final conversation. And even though we share tips for better conversations at the end of each chapter and will suggest useful communication skills in the final chapter, we must be honest: We don't have a formula for the perfect goodbye, because there isn't one. There are many. Each will look and sound different. What the Living who speak in these chapters propose is to accept what you can do and what your loved one can do. No matter what you expect, the actual experience will always unfold differently.

According to Laurie, it simply isn't your plan to make. The best you can do is to deal with how it all rolls out. *Even though I had prepared knowing she was dying, I could tell anyone this: you could prepare in your mind, but it never, ever goes how you think it's gonna go. In fact, it's worse if you prepare, because then when it doesn't happen the way you thought it should, you don't know how to react because it's not going according to your plan.*

Laurie then told us about how her plan fell apart. *Nothing went according to plan. It just didn't. I had specifically told my mom that I didn't want to see an open casket. And we talked about this when she was in the hospital on a previous visit some time before. She told me, "You know, I never wanted to see my mother either, but I did. And afterwards I visited with several of her friends, and they told me how comforting it was for them to see her one last time and to say goodbye." I do remember this conversation real specifically, because I answered back very quickly, "Well, that was great for them, but as I'm saying, it's not what I wanna do."*

Then the time came; her mother died, and Laurie had to make arrangements for her funeral. *So, I had picked up her clothes and sent them with my brother to the funeral home. They had called and said, "Do you want to come down and see how all the clothes worked out?" I said, "Sure, I'll go down." So, Charles and I go down to the funeral home. And I walk into this room where there's an open casket and I turn and walk out. I said, "No, no, no. I didn't say that I was gonna look at her in the clothes. I just wanted to see how the clothes laid out." They said, "Well, that's what this is about. You need to do this, but if you don't want to, I'll take care of it." Then I said, "No, I wanna see how she looks. I picked out the clothes. I wanna know." I went up and she looked beautiful. I'm glad I did it because she looked so bad in her last few days. It wasn't how she would've wanted anyone to remember her. She looked amazing. There were a couple of things that weren't right. Her lipstick wasn't right. So, I took a lip liner out of my purse and touched it up 'cause that's how she wore her lipstick.*

For a woman who never wanted to see her mother after her death, Laurie did a complete turnabout to actually assisting with her makeup and clothes. Once you can release the need for control that is often born of fear, it becomes possible to allow yourself the privilege of just assisting in the process as you are needed. This kind of release is not only a gift to the Dying but also a blessing for the Living.

No Fear, No Regrets

One typical response to engaging with the Dying is a lessening of the fear the Living carry about death. Her grandmother's death not only emboldened Breanna to place her own needs in a priority position above others, but it has also changed her feeling about death. *I'm not afraid of death anymore. I wasn't afraid of being near her or what was happening—I mean I was afraid—but it just seemed natural. I was there when she died, and that made a big, big impact on me. Because she died and I was there right beside her and it didn't seem scary at all. It seemed almost beautiful in the way that it happened. I think that changes you. I was very happy that I had been with her the last two days—it meant a lot to me. Because of this experience, I'm more accepting of death. It's not so horrific.*

Particularly for those who may not say all they need to say, or for those who fail to have the talks at all, regrets can loom large after the Dying is gone. What should I have said? What should I have expressed? Did they die as they wanted? Grace had begun to have these thoughts about her husband's death, but upon reflection, she finds no reason for regret.

As any person in a situation where you're the final caregiver, you question whether or not you did enough. You question your own actions. You question your own conversations. You question whether you told them enough that they were loved and whether you listened enough to their feelings, and whether you were projecting your feelings onto them more than you should have. And I think that gave me some self-doubt. I had to sit down and examine what I had done and what I should have done. And that caused me to eliminate the word should *from my conversations with anybody or from my thoughts. I came to the conclusion that I had done the best I could at the moment. What I thought was the best I could give. There was nothing that I should've done, that I could've done otherwise.*

Changes in attitude often lead to changes in behavior. For some of the Living, these shifts lead them to new ways of thinking about and acting in relationships. For others, they may lead to new directions in education, career, and personal passions to contribute to society, to serve others.

NEW PLANS, NEW PATHS

When you no longer have someone watching over your life, you must care enough about yourself to finally do what others may have urged you to do before—do well in school, choose a career, a vocation, find fulfillment, find love.

Time to Take Charge of My Life

Judy's sister decided in middle age to take their biological father's last name, which Judy saw as a slap to Frank, the stepdad who'd taken care of them and provided a real home as they grew up. That spurred Judy to write Frank a long letter to tell him all the things she appreciated about him. She subsequently spent time with him and felt complete. Frank was her last link to a nurturing parent; both her biological parents died before Frank. Judy called him her "spare" parent. And then he was dying, and she was truly an orphaned adult. *That's my last parent to die. Well, I've always thought that would be really scary, but he lived so long, and I lived so long with him, that for me it's like I'm not alone. It's a freedom to continue. It's not like there's nothing between me and death. It's more like, it's up to me to take charge of my life. He's always there in the back of my mind.* Judy felt a new impetus to move into full adulthood with Frank's death. She was truly independent now and answerable only to herself.

Relationships: Cherish Your Intimates and Love Again

Relationships often take unexpected twists and turns. Some we take for granted because we expect that they will always be there, and some surprise us. And there are those who think that it will be impossible to ever love again. These final conversations show us the bittersweet nature of relationships, as well as the gifts of awareness, honesty, and the power of permission to go on loving and living following the death of a loved one.

In our culture it is commonplace to take relationships for granted. We work ourselves silly, assuming that friends and family will be there waiting for us when we're done—if ever we're done. When Sam's mother died, he learned something about *that whole idea of living your life with anticipation of checking out of this world. You can be facing your death with fear, denial, a feeling of emptiness or loneliness; or you can be prepared for it. The way you prepare yourself is by making decisions in life leading up to it. So, integrity and the decisions that you make about what's really important, like family—spending time with family versus things like money—that's probably the biggest part of it. I think if I were summarizing all of the reminiscing—the things that she remembered in the end of her life, some of which were very mundane—those were the things that were really important. It was family, it was relationships. That was really it.*

Carol agrees that final conversations open the Living to people in general and family in particular. *I tried since then to be more honest about what I'm thinking or feeling with those that I love and care about and not to let things go. What I learned has to do with: Why waste all that time not being close? I think, in general, I am a lot more open and straight with people up front. I tend to be a pretty private person, I think. But in the last year I've seen a shift where I'll talk more openly about a whole realm of things that I would not have a year earlier. It's because I want to know people better and I have, I think, more realization that I might not have another opportunity to.*

Helen and Ramona were best friends for 20 years before becoming partners for one year before she was diagnosed with lung cancer. Upon getting together as partners, Helen said, *"I always thought I was getting you ready for someone else, with these conversations of getting you to accept yourself and come out to yourself. I didn't realize I was getting you ready for me." Then when she was in her final weeks of living, we took a drive. Helen said, "You're going to have a lot of changes coming up in the future." I said, "You mean because of you and your illness." She said, "Yes." I asked, "What do you want from me, hon?" She said, "I want you to be happy, to live for yourself and not for what others think you should do or how you should be." Then she continued, "I guess it goes back to what I said all along." I asked, "What is that?" She said, "I guess I was getting you ready for someone else." I was speechless. She died about five weeks after being diagnosed with stage 4 lung cancer.*

The Dying often know better than those they leave behind just how much the Living will need close relationships. Even though no one is replaceable, especially intimates, spouses especially seem concerned that the Living love again. Sondra's husband made clear that he wanted her to remarry after his death. *Life goes on. There is certainly a time that you do miss that person. Gosh, the loneliness I felt after that was extreme. But those conversations with Steve always reminded me that life does get better, and life does go on. I knew that for me to remarry was what he wanted. And that conversation definitely had an impact. The man I'm married to now, Glen, he had a very similar conversation with his late wife: "I want you to remarry." I think even with both of us today, we both know that we had the blessing of our previous spouses, our late spouses. That conversation had a big impact on why we don't have that bitterness, or don't have that mourning and grief. Yeah, there's times when we miss them and those memories do come back.* But their spouses made it possible for them to go on, to love again, to benefit from the closest of relationships.

The Living find that communicating with the Dying reminds them of the importance of close relationships in their lives, motivates them to pay more attention to and be more honest with their friends and family, and focuses them on the gift of finding love again. Some of the same Living also found new directions for their personal achievements.

Education: New Personal Goals

Not all the Living who spoke of their renewed dedication to study were traditional, college-age students. After her son died—as a young man who never got the chance to continue his education—Gloria went back to school. In part, she credits her son for her inspiration. *He said, "Mom, I want you to go back to school. That's where you belong. You and I need to be lawyers. So that way we can help people, help children, help women." He said, "I want you to go back to school." And I told him, "With everything that's happened, Jacob, I don't know if I can." He goes, "Mom, just go. What did you tell me, Mom, when we first found out that I have leukemia? You said we're fighters. You're a fighter, Mom. You're the one who taught us how to be this way." And he said, "I want you to go back to school, Mom."*

Following Jacob's death, Gloria worked full time while completing her bachelor's degree with a major in political science. Upon graduation she got a new job working for Child Protective Services as an advocate for children. Jacob and his mother were alike in many ways, not the least of which was their willingness to serve others. And in some way, Jacob's idealism will live on in his mother's work.

Career: New Contributions

The Living may continue in their current jobs with a new view of how they want to do it, or they may quit doing what they have no passion for and create new paths. After her mother's death, Lorie not only slowed down the pace of her stressful life but embarked on work that would allow her to reflect on what she did. *So, I try to be a little more mindful and have a little more time to, I don't know, meditate, for lack of a better word. Just quietly think about what's going on. It's a good lesson. I was very caught up in my life.*

It did change how I view work. I quit working for corporate America and went out on my own. It's been scary, but the way things happened with my mother still provides me with a little income that tided me over—something I never could've done without that. Not only did her mother's death spur her to consider more how she was spending her life, but it also provided the means for her to do so. Perhaps not everyone will be as fortunate, but everyone can consider whether the work they do suits their life goals.

Emily said goodbye to her best friend, Jeanette, decades ago; she became a hospice volunteer following Jeanette's death. Her friend did not have the kind of support Emily wanted her to have, so she searched for the beginnings of the hospice movement in this country. And found it. She counseled the Living to interact with the Dying for many years. *Her death made me really want to take the hospice training.*

After she completed her training and began to work, she started having experiences that told her she was doing the right thing; work aligned with her passion and talent. Emily saw the need and recognized her own place in the world. She honored her friend's memory by dedicating the rest of her life to helping others die. It is work in which she clearly found delight and fulfillment, and a way to keep the memory of her friend alive.

SUMMARY

Basically, the effects of final conversations on the rest of the Living's days can be boiled down to two broad effects: loosening up and resetting life's defaults. But these two forces can create huge shifts in attitudes, relationships, and vocation.

Loosening Up

Yes, that's a pretty broad statement. "Loosening up" means taking yourself and every single limitation you perceive in your life less seriously. The Living learned to stop walking on eggshells and to say what they needed to say. They learned to take the time from their serious daily lives to be with the Dying. They learned to break the rules—the cultural norms and the family regulations—in order to do what they felt they must do. And they learned to let go of control, both over the process of the Dying and over their own emotions and actions. Isn't this all about loosening up and letting it happen? Sure. Is it easy to do? No, but take hope from those who were able to do it. You will be reminded of your own mortality. And you will be able to give yourself permission to do what your heart tells you to do.

Resetting Life's Defaults

People walk through many of their days on autopilot. And that works for us. We'd never get through repetitive daily tasks without default settings—the automatic drive that allows us to do things without thinking about them. Take driving to work. Aren't there days when you scarcely are conscious of where you have been until you pull into the plant parking lot? But, if there's an accident on the way, you have no trouble switching to a highly conscious mode of thinking. In that case, you can vividly describe to your spouse that night what happened around you and your responses to it.

Similarly, the walk through life can get pretty programmed. You're supposed to go to school, you're supposed to make a good living, you're supposed to keep in touch—minimally—with family. So, you do. But if you sleepwalk through life—and most do to some extent—there will come a day when you are jogged out of that sleep into an awareness that this life may come to an end tomorrow. That's when the sleepwalking ends, at least for a while. The Living tell us that after you engage with someone whom you've counted on to be there, that you are forced to think about your loss. And that leads you to rethink your family relationships, your friends, your loves. It leads you to value them more and take them for granted less. Or it leads you to make changes in your relationship choices, and in what you expect from a close relationship. For many, it will mean re-evaluating the way you spend your days and, consequently, changing occupations, going back to school, or revising the time spent making money. In other words, final conversations can lead to resetting the defaults of life.

The death of your loved one is going to change you and your life. Final conversations simply allow the Dying to help guide you onto the new path.

TIPS FOR BETTER CONVERSATIONS

Before the Death:

- Do whatever is necessary to spend time with the Dying. Speak with your boss, your colleagues, your friends, and family to see if they can help you break away from your daily schedule. Be the caregiver if you are able, even if it isn't expected of you.

- Break the rules! Defy ordinary conventions or habitual norms to say what you need to say. Dying is not an ordinary, everyday experience for you or your loved one. Find your feelings and then find your voice.
- Confront your fear of death. Interacting with the Dying will help to dissipate that fear.
- Let the communications unfold as they will. They aren't yours to control or even to prepare. Just prepare yourself to *be there*. Keep in mind that showing up is half the battle. The other half of success may be listening carefully. See the final chapter for details.

After the Death:

- Give yourself permission to grieve. Grief comes in waves that gradually become less turbulent. If you are having difficulty moving through the grief, seek a grief counselor you feel comfortable with.
- If you are comfortable sharing personal stories about your final conversations with others whom you trust—especially after you have done much of your grieving—do so. It is a way to learn more about the messages after you have some time to reflect.
- Value your own spirit as well as others'. Don't put off treating yourself and others compassionately.
- See where your own attitude shifts take you in life. Follow your own good impulses. No one else can show you your way.
- Find life's joy. It is unlimited, but your time on earth is not.

chapter 14

The Conversation Continues Beyond Death

Why is Mom in this dream? She doesn't belong in this setting. I remember asking: "Why did you come now?" And Pat said, "Because you needed me, and I'll try to come whenever you need me." (Colleen)

Over the past 20 years many have told us about signs, sensory experiences, and dreams they have received from their loved ones who have crossed over. Sometimes they appear within days, but more often weeks, months, and years following the death. These experiences did not frighten them; rather they gave them hope that a connection between them would continue, that their deceased loved ones were watching over them, and that they would see them again. They brought them joy and release from their grief.

DEATH DOES NOT END THE RELATIONSHIP

One thing we know for sure after studying relationships for so long is that they do not suddenly end. Whether you leave a friendship, go through a divorce, or grieve the death of a family member, the relationship continues in the symbols you've shared. While creating close human connections, we come to share meaning for the words we use, the gestures we make, the objects we gift, the experiences we go through together. And those meanings do not just vanish. Even damaging relationships leave us with lingering meanings that tell us what we do and don't want. The meanings we create with those most cherished stay with us forever. The departed may return via those shared meanings in real-time experience and in the dreamtime.

REAL-TIME MESSAGES

Real-time messages from loved ones who have crossed over are those that we perceive during everyday life. It is a familiar touch, a glimpse of their face, the smell of their perfume, a bird that keeps returning, the lights that flicker when you call their name. These extraordinary stories are of physical events that were understood by the Living as meaningful connections to their departed loved ones. They are tangible, profound, and unexplainable except for the belief that it was the departed reaching out to them.

Sensory Experiences

Touch. Ellen had asked Michael to reach out to her after his death to let her know they were still connected. *I told him that I needed him to somehow, somewhere along the line, to make contact with me. I said you just have to do this. Some time had already passed, and I was just in agony. I missed him so much.* Finally, Ellen felt Michael's presence. *I was driving around with the radio on, and I wasn't thinking about Michael. There was nothing going on in my mind that was connected to him at all. Suddenly, I felt Michael's hand touch my right shoulder. First, you have to get that Michael was 6'5 1/2". I am a small-boned, tiny woman; I am 5'2". Okay? So, when he would have put his hand on my shoulder, his hand covered my entire shoulder. It was his touch. I mean, I was married to the man for a long time; it was Michael. I immediately turned my head to the passenger-side seat because that's how strong the feeling was. Of course, nobody was there. And it was like, "Oh, my God. What was that? What could that be?" It was part of my education that communication is really possible.*

Vision. When Jane's youngest son, Michael, died at 37 years old, Jane almost died herself. When she heard the news, she suffered "broken heart syndrome" and was rushed to the hospital. After time spent in the intensive care unit, she survived, but her grief remained with her. Tragically, about a decade later, her older son, Matt, died, at 49 years old, a week after a medical procedure. Jane was deep in grief. One day, a few months after his death, as she was sitting on her couch in her living room, she saw Matt standing a few feet away, coming into the living room. He said to her, *"Mom, I want you to know that I am good, that I am here with Michael, and we are surrounded by love."* This experience changed everything for Jane; she found a new sense of peace.

Scent. The departed may use this sense to stir memories of them. For Patty, the scents came unbidden to remind her of loved ones gone. Patty knew that she was going to lose her daughter-in-law, who had been fighting a rare form of cancer. *My heart was heavy as I thought about the impending loss my son and his family would be facing. I was driving to visit her and feeling bereft in the knowledge of her losing battle. Suddenly I thought, I want my mother. It was a powerful yearning, and the force of it surprised me. And almost immediately the car was filled with the scent of my mother. It was visceral. It was the smell I remembered as a little girl, a mixture of cooking smells, her perfume, and smoky smells, for she was a smoker in my younger years. And in that car, for that brief time, my mother came to comfort me.*

Sound. Patty shared one more story with us that involved the sound of her grandparents' as well as scent. *My first husband and I were just married (1972) and renting my grandparents' house. All summer we had been stripping wallpaper, sanding floors, and painting woodwork. I had mixed feelings as we turned what was their home into what was to be our home. I felt as if I was hurting their feelings. One night I woke in the middle of the night to the particular smell that had always been at my grandparents' house upon entering it. The paint and varnish smells were gone. And there at the foot of the bed they were; I could not see them, but I heard these words from them: "We are happy you are here." I felt a great peace and drifted back to sleep. The paint and varnish smells returned the next morning, and I never smelled that particular grandparents'-house smell again.*

Signs from the Departed

The Living sometimes requested that the departed send a sign that they were still with them. At other times, the signs came unbidden. They shared stories of meaningful objects appearing in unusual places, particular birds or flowers emerging with uncanny consistency or timing, electric objects turning on by themselves at moments when the loved one was mentioned. The Living found no plausible explanation for these phenomena other than that their departed loved one was making their presence known.

Meaningful Objects. Maureen shared an experience that showed her that her mother was still checking in and watching over her and her family. Six months after her death, her father, twin sister, niece, and nephew came to visit her from out of town. *I had gotten up early to get ready for work and had jumped into the shower. I looked down at my hand and realized that my mother's diamond engagement ring was not on my finger (I recently had it reset and resized into a yellow gold band). In a panic, I quickly turned off the shower and went to wake up my husband to help me look in the drain for it. As I opened the bathroom door into our bedroom, the light focused on my side of the bed, and on the floor laid the ring. It was as if I had slept with my hand hanging over the bed and it had slipped off my finger—except that the ring was sized for a tight fit and it was difficult to pull off. I also sleep on my side with my hand under my pillow. I put the ring back on and went to work. Later that day upon my return home, I shared the story with my family. My dad remarked, "That's funny, I had the most wonderful dream that your mother came and kissed me, and I woke up feeling her lips on mine!" My sister and I said, "Dad, that's because she did come and kiss you, and she is the one who took off the diamond ring to let us know that she was there with us!"*

Tansy shared several occurrences involving significant objects that happened following the death of Eli, her eight-year-old son. These two are special. *Over the first couple months after his death, he worked overtime to let me know he was okay, and we could still have a relationship. It would just look a little bit different. A week after he passed, I went to the mailbox, as it was overflowing. I got all the mail and proceeded to turn away, when out of the corner of my eye, I saw a bunch of multicolored Legos, one of his favorite toys, on the ground right in front of our box. They had not been there the previous day.*

A month later, right before Valentine's Day, I decided I was going to attempt to make cupcakes. Baking usually was comforting, and I thought this might help me in some little way. I opened the cupboard to get out the baking pan I needed. When taking it out, underneath and behind it was a handwritten card I had never seen before. It looked like something he would have made in school. It said, "Mom: I love you to pieces [with glued-on puzzle pieces on it]. Eli." I had never seen this card before. We have so many stories to tell of instances like this. They all lead us to believe, beyond a shadow of a doubt, that Eli lives on and is always with us.

Signs in the Natural World: Birds, Butterflies, Flowers. We often are inspired by nature, in simple and profound ways. Quite a few of the Living shared stories of noticing odd regularities in the natural world that they concluded were beyond mere coincidence. Carissa told us that there are many times that she has felt her brother Bradley nearby or was given a visual reminder that he is with her. This is especially true on the anniversary of his death at age nine. *Every year on August 19, I see a hawk or have an unusual encounter with one. I know it sounds strange, but it's true, and why hawks? I have no idea! I'm not even sure if Bradley liked hawks. From an incident of a hawk flying with me six inches directly above my head as I was water skiing, to one almost crashing into my windshield, to one sitting on my pergola or front porch, or circling above my house every year on August 19. The latest gift was given shortly before my dad passed away. My dad kept talking to Bradley and calling his name, and moments before he took his last breath, his eyes opened wide; he got this huge smile across his face as he said, "Oh, it's you!" Later that afternoon, after my dad passed, my aunt told me, "The strangest thing happened today. When I got back to your dad's house, there were seven hawks lined up and sitting on his fence." I just smiled, looked up, and said thank you!*

Just a few years ago, Susu's beloved husband, Howard, died from an aggressive cancer that he fought for six weeks before he succumbed to the disease. She shared that *upon his final moments, his brother whispered in his ear, "Come and give me a sign to let me know you are home." That same afternoon, he witnessed a butterfly landing on his beer; then it moved to flutter around his head; just after that, he fluttered into the house and actually landed on my hand—the same butterfly, with my son capturing a photo of the wink.* Butterflies are now frequent sightings. One time Susu and her sons were driving on a road trip and their car was swarmed with butterflies. Another time, she and a friend were watching a movie and noticed *that a small butterfly had actually landed on the ceiling fan in the living room. Without warning, the fan turned on by itself, making the butterfly fly around the room. We know that it is Howard every time butterflies come into our lives in extraordinary ways!*

Flowers have special significance in many relationships. Patty's story is about lilies. *During my mother's later years on earth, my sisters and I frequently gave her lilies on Easter. After many years of receiving them and then planting the bulbs to no avail, she finally said, "I don't know why you girls keep giving me these Easter lilies, because they never come back." Our mother was a very straightforward person. After she died, I missed her terribly. The hole that was left was simply gaping. And then one summer day of that same year, I was surveying my stone-walled garden, and there in the far corner was a beautiful pure white Easter lily in full bloom. I had never planted any Easter lily bulbs in my garden. There was no doubt in my mind that it was from my mother letting me know that she was alright. And maybe she was even a little apologetic after her chastisement of our many gifts of Easter lilies.*

Nudges to Remind Us: Moving Memories and Flickering Lights. Sometimes the sign is more mechanical rather than natural, although the butterfly on the ceiling fan managed to do both! Sometimes these are just winks and nods, but sometimes they come with gifts.

Celinda shared a special story about her daughter with us: *Since the loss of my precious Audrey, I have received many messages, and all have been significant and comforting—no matter how large or small—I know she is there, and it warms my shattered and broken heart.* Audrey reached out to Celinda's friend Julie to get a message to her mom. *A few months after the service, Julie was working on a complicated jigsaw puzzle of Cinque Terre, Italy. Julie says that while working on the puzzle, she had placed a copy of Audrey's funeral program on her bar, and suddenly, the program flew off of her bar and landed atop the puzzle of Cinque Terre. She snapped a photo, simply to tell me that the funeral program had somehow blown on top of where she was working, thinking Audrey was trying to get her attention. She was, but Julie did not know the significance of Cinque Terre. When I noticed the steps of Cinque Terre peeking out from under the program, I sent her my favorite photo of Audrey in Italy. It was taken at a terrace restaurant overlooking the magnificent, romantic city of Cinque Terre. Julie was completely blown away. In turn she sent me a photo of the puzzle, and sure enough, it was Cinque Terre. "I believe this is a sign from Audrey—a sign that she is here, there, and especially Cinque Terre," Julie wrote. "Absolutely extraordinary!"*

Karly, a reflexologist, had worked closely for years with an elderly couple, John and Jenny, toward the end of each of their lives. *After attending their mother's funeral and meeting all the faces that belonged to the stories I had heard about over the years, I let the daughters know Jenny had two paid sessions left. I gave them the option of reflexology gift certificates or a return of the money. The daughters chose to receive reflexology. The first daughter had lived next door, so it was very easy to schedule her session.*

The second daughter, coming from out-of-state, called within the next few months and explained that she would be in the area cleaning out her mother's house. She said that she would like to use the gift certificate. It happened to be the day I would have been in the area to work on her mother. As the main floor had already been emptied, we went upstairs. She explained that she had grown up in this house. We went to her old bedroom, and I pulled a chair up to the foot of the bed to do the foot reflexology. As the session began, I was embarrassed by the music CD that kept cutting out like it had a scratch in it. We couldn't get the music to play right, so we turned it off. It was when the lamp started flickering that I thought maybe we weren't alone. I stopped and said I just feel like your mother is here. "Me too," she said. I can then only describe this feeling as a "knowing" and I asked, "Is it your birthday?" I added, "Your mother is giving you reflexology for your birthday." "Yes," she replied with a surprised look. "It is my birthday!" Now, how I knew that was beyond me. It was exactly the classy move Judy would have done. "You want to hear something else weird?" she asked. "Of course, I do." "Every year growing up my mother would leave me a gift at the foot of my bed." There I sat at the foot of her bed. I was giving her a reflexology birthday gift from her mom who was still watching over her. These little mechanical glitches that make us pay attention may serve to remind us that the departed would like to continue giving as they did in life.

Near-Death Contact. We received quite a few stories from the Living who had been either very ill, hurt in an accident, or facing imminent death, and were assisted by a departed loved one. Stories about our loved ones watching over us and protecting us from the other side are beautiful and intense. These stories are often life changing.

Elaine experienced the grace of a departed friend's presence when she was very sick and alone in an ambulance and emergency room. *In early July at the height of the COVID pandemic, I became ill, with some symptoms like COVID. No one in my doctor's office would see me. A week passes, I'm getting sicker—it's affecting my brain. I'm not thinking clearly, and I have trouble focusing. My husband finally says, "That's it! I'm taking you to the hospital." Once there, I was diagnosed with babesiosis, a deer tick-borne disease that attacks the red blood cells. The ER doctor decided it would be best if I was treated at a larger hospital and had an ambulance transport me to it. I was conscious enough to express my dismay—this hospital ER has a reputation as a zoo.*

I'm in the ambulance and become aware of a presence with me. A woman's voice is consoling me as we ride to the hospital. When we arrive, I'm wheeled into the ER, where there are many patients waiting, moaning, crying, even someone shouting. My "companion" is outraged, telling me that this is unacceptable, and that I need to be moved out of this place. Of course, there's nothing I can do about it. In what seemed to me to be a short amount of time, an attendant came to me and said that he was moving me to a quiet area. To this day I believe that my "angel companion" convinced this man to move me. He put me in an unused exam room, away from the waiting room. At some point I was moved up to a room in the hospital. My "angel companion" stayed with me the whole time, sometimes talking, encouraging me. Even when she wasn't talking, I felt her presence. We entered my room. There was a large sign on the wall about a telephone being made available and to ask about how to get it. My "angel" pointed the sign out and told me to be sure to ask about the phone in the morning. When I was transferred from the gurney to the bed, I realized she was gone.

The next morning, I wondered who she was. At first, I thought of my mother, then realized the voice and the attitude were not those of my mother. It was my dear friend Marie, who had died over a decade earlier. In the moment when Elaine could not think clearly, she was just grateful for the companion who helped her. When her mind started to clear, she knew who her companion had been in her time of need.

Marian, an avid scuba diver for over 15 years, would share pictures, videos, and stories with her mother, Marilyn, about her scuba diving adventures. Marilyn often expressed fear about her daughter's adventures. After Marilyn's death, Marian had an experience that confirmed her mother's fears. During a diving trip with her husband, she had trouble with her equipment that almost took her life. *I have my own equipment and get it inspected regularly, so I never have any real concerns about it working. However, on my "check-out" dive, my equipment seemed to malfunction. My BCD [buoyancy control device—or buoyancy life jacket] kept filling with air—shooting me to the surface of the water. No matter how often I emptied the air, it filled again. So, it was like I was on a bungee cord, rapidly going up and down, and making me motion sick. After 10 minutes of this, I became extremely nauseous and started throwing up in my mask. My husband was with me and recognized something was wrong. He grabbed my BCD and began dragging me to the surface. As we were underwater, we could not communicate, but he knew I was struggling. As he was pulling me, I began choking and thinking I might never draw another breath of air again.*

I recall thinking, "Oh my God . . . this is the way it ends!" As I was thinking this, my mom's voice immediately popped into my head. It was so loud*! She was literally screaming at me; I could hear her perfectly, and she was saying, "Marian,* calm down*; stop fighting!" I remember asking, "What? Mom, is that you?" She continued yelling. In fact, she yelled "Marian,* calm down*!" all the way to the shore. We were out in the lagoon approximately 200 yards; that was a lot of dragging for my husband and so much hollering from my mom. But her words buoyed me. I suddenly pulled my face out of the water and calmly told my husband to stop pulling me, that I could swim the rest of the distance. I told him Mom was there, and as she did when I would become upset as a child, she told me to calm down. He believed me and stopped swimming. I swam the rest of the way. I made it into shore and thanked Mom—I knew she was there, and she reminded me I was strong, and my emotions were preventing me from using my knowledge and skills. She saved me—plain and simple. She has always known me so well and knows what it always took to get me to listen.*

My mom was right there when I needed her. She sensed it and she spoke directly to me. I tell everyone this story. Some friends give me a crazy, quizzical stare. That is fine. I don't care what they believe; I am the luckiest person to still have her with me.

DREAMTIME MESSAGES

Most of us have dreams every night, although we often don't remember them. Dreams about our loved ones can vary from a sweet memory of our departed, to dreams that feel like the person is in the room with them, hugging them, talking to them, comforting them, or sometimes warning them. These dreams feel real and are reported as visits from the departed. The dreams shared with us are filled with vivid descriptions of affection and welcome messages. Sometimes the departed will come to us in dreams when we need them but may not be open to a real-time experience. In the last example, a dream leads into a real-time vision. Often, at the threshold of the dream world, we are more open to a real-time connection and can take it in, if only briefly.

Dreams with Specific Messages

"I Am Sorry I Had to Leave." Nikkie didn't have to wait long for the dream of her husband, Les. *Following his death, I was hoping to see him in my dreams, and a few nights after his wake, I felt his presence in my dream. This dream felt so real. He called my name until I listened while in the dream, and then he said, "Nikkie, I am so sorry that I had to leave so soon." I could see him so clearly in my dream as if he were alive. The dream woke me, and my heart was beating so quickly. In that dream he looked peaceful but was so apologetic. His gentle voice was so clear, and he hoped that I would understand. I dreamt about Les a few times after that dream, always with that beautiful smile, but that first dream was the most impactful because it was so soon after his passing and with such an important message.*

"I Am Waiting for Her." Franny shared a dream she had about her father. *I had my last conversation with my dad about two weeks after he died. He was diagnosed in early May and passed away on July 1 at about* *sunset. My siblings and my mom were there with me as his breathing stopped with a final sigh. Heartbroken, we all struggled through the funeral and burial. When it was all over, I was tormented by the unanswered questions of what happened to this wonderful man after death, what happened to the spirit that was my dad for almost 80 years. I should not have worried, because shortly after, I had a very vivid dream. Unlike the myriad of dreams I have conjured in the years before and after, it was not a muddle of images nor a whirling panorama of motion and sound. This dream was remarkable because it was so detailed and specific. I was touring the Breakers mansion in Newport with my sisters and my mother. We were following a tour guide from the music room into the morning room when I saw my father standing outside on the stone patio. Dad often chauffeured my mom to the market or picked her up after work. He would arrive early and stand near the car with his fingers linked behind him rocking back and forth, from heel to toe, watching people and cars go by. He was doing just that when I slipped through the door away from the tour and began speaking before I even reached him. "What are you doing here, Dad?" He replied, "Waiting for your mother." I asked him, "Should I tell her you are here?" He told me, "No, no need. She doesn't have to come now. I'm just here waiting for her and will be here when it's her time." He looked healthy again and he was at peace. He urged me to catch up with my group, and when I stepped inside and looked back, he was gone. I am convinced that the dead do visit the Living to help heal our broken hearts.*

Dreams That Bring Peace

"I Love You Still." Kay shared with us a dream about one of her best friends, Lyle, two months following his death. The images and message in the dream provided comfort and explanation following a strained ending to their 37-year friendship. *I am with Lyle. He takes me into an embrace, my head resting on his chest. He is warm and kind. Then he and I are swimming in dark, opaque water and he is talking about growing up, being gay, and how careful he had to be and how much he had to learn.* This dream was important to Kay, because it told her that their friendship and love remained and that he was finally at peace with his true self.

"Don't Worry; I Am Fine." When Carissa was 13 years old, she was severely injured and her 9-year-old brother was killed in a car crash involving a drunk driver. She shared this story with us about dream visits with him. *Bradley would visit me often in my dreams for the first two years following his death. I always had the same dream. We would be in the back of a car riding through the hill country, and I couldn't believe he was there with me. I was so happy. We would hug and talk about how good it was to see each other. He would tell me that he was fine, I didn't need to worry or be sad, and that where he was, was so beautiful. One night after the dream, he told me that I could go with him, so I started to follow him. I turned around and could see myself asleep in my bed, but something wouldn't let me go. I woke up abruptly, a little shaken and saddened that the dream was over. I was a sweaty mess, so I went to the kitchen to get a glass of water. In our house, there was a huge mirror clock on the wall that you had to pass to get to the kitchen. As I passed by the clock, I saw his reflection right behind me. I stopped and stared, blinked a few times in disbelief, rubbed my eyes, stared longer, and finally turned around, but when I did, he was gone. This was probably the biggest gift of his presence I ever received.*

Dreams are a wonderful way to connect with our loved ones who have died. They are not scary or disturbing; in fact, everyone who shared their stories with us told us how much lighter they felt, as if some of their heavy grief had lifted, and they generally woke feeling happy and comforted.

SUMMARY

Continuing the conversation beyond the deaths of loved ones is a way to continue our relationships with them, to help us feel close to them, to feel comforted that they are observing what is going on in our lives. We can't prove their empirical reality, and we are not trying to convince anyone that they should interpret these events in the same way. We simply believe the experiences of the Living who shared their stories with us. Some connect with departed loved ones in *real-time* through sensory perception, events in nature that seem to be more than coincidence, and odd glitches in machinery we use daily. Some connect in *dreamtime*, either receiving direct messages from their loved ones or a general sense of peace. We hope that you treasure those messages from beyond that you are fortunate enough to receive.

TIPS FOR BETTER CONVERSATIONS

- If you wish to connect with your departed loved one, keep asking them to visit you. Be patient and trust that it will happen—often when you least expect it.
- If your departed loved one pops into your head out of the blue, trust that they are nearby and thank them for reminding you of their presence.
- If you believe a sign such as the appearance of a butterfly, a dragonfly, or a specific type of bird represents your loved one, then accept this gift and respond in your own way.
- If you haven't had a sign, or experience from your departed loved one, perhaps they aren't ready to come to you yet. Many departed souls take some time to adjust to being back on the other side. Or perhaps you want to believe that it is possible, but you're doubtful and not fully open to the experience, which can block their communication to you from the other side. The departed may find it easier to reach you via dreams. You may want to remind yourself as you go to sleep that you wish to remember your dreams.
- Dreams of our deceased loved ones can be clear and precise, or they can be confusing and out of context. Our loved ones can pop into dreams when they see an opportunity to reach us, but they may be in a situation where they shouldn't be, or in the middle of a scene that wouldn't be possible if they were alive. Sometimes the details in the dream are important because they are a part of the message, whereas other times it is simply seeing, hugging, or hearing a message from our departed loved one that is important. You are the expert on what is relevant and important in your dream. Consider writing down vivid dreams so you can consider what they mean for you.

part four

YOUR FINAL CONVERSATIONS

chapter 15

We Never Said It Was Easy

It feels surreal. You don't fully understand the big picture. The most challenging thing was you knew it was happening but didn't think it actually would. Today I can remember more than I thought I ever would, but right when it happened, I was completely numb. (Joshua)

Final conversations are challenging. Heightened emotions may include apprehension, fear, and uncertainty as well as the grief that may begin even before death. Many conversations are delayed by denial, by the perceived need to stifle uncomfortable emotions, by the feeling that the time is too limited and is running out. In this chapter, we want to share with you some of the challenges that the Living shared with us as they faced their own final conversations with the Dying. In reading these stories, we hope you will realize that you are not alone, that you can overcome the anxiety that you may be feeling, and that you can rise above any obstacles that you may face.

AVOIDING FINAL CONVERSATIONS

Avoidance of these interactions often pops up in the false belief that if you don't participate in them, then you can keep hope alive and stall death. The medical care system fosters this false hope by delaying death using experimental treatments and life-support systems. The Living often choose to focus on potential medical miracles to avoid the reality of what that loss means to their life and ultimately to avoid final conversations. Tara told us: *My experience was one of obstinate refusal to believe I was having final conversations.* Sometimes the Dying is ready, willing, and able to communicate at the end of life, but the Living ignores the obvious physical signs of the body declining and chats idly with the Dying without truly acknowledging the deterioration, thus limiting their interactions. Colin said, *I didn't want to believe she was dying. I wonder if I didn't visit and call more because I didn't want to have it confirmed that she was getting worse.* His refusal to accept the approaching death meant that he had fewer talks with his mother. Katy expressed the regret that comes with avoidance. *I was in denial that death was coming as soon as it did, so I did not say everything I now wish I had. I was left with regrets of unexpressed affection and interest.*

Gillian offers multiple reasons for avoiding interactions with the Dying that include denial that death will happen, life circumstances, and a lack of time. *I was in denial to some extent and believed she would come home from the hospital. I had a one-year-old baby, and my aunt didn't want me to come to the hospital very much in case I exposed my daughter to any illnesses. I was also a working mother at the time. I used these reasons to some extent to avoid the pain of what was inevitable. I was left with guilt and regret after the death.* There is no way to sugar-coat it; watching someone you love deteriorating and dying is *hard.* We also know that *not* having these conversations is harder in the long run. Just ask someone whose loved one died suddenly and who had no opportunity for final conversations.

OBSTACLES TO FINAL CONVERSATIONS

Some of the Living avoided topics that they perceived might be challenging, difficult, or negative for the Dying. Some felt that their conversations were restricted because of a lack of privacy. Others thought they needed to hide their real emotions during their interactions for a variety of reasons. And several people felt that the pressure of time negatively influenced their final conversations. For others, the limits to communication arose from the Dying's medical condition, the restrictions of living far away, or hindrances of technology. Finally, there are a few obstacles unique to individuals that may make participating in final conversations more challenging.

Topics Avoided

The Living avoided conversational topics that had the potential to make a difficult situation more tense or damaging. Heston shared that he did not bring up his *father's prejudices and how it strained the relationship. I also didn't talk about the negative things in our relationship because at that moment and under those circumstances I didn't want to bring up or address anything bad. It wasn't going to change anything by this point, and it could make him feel worse when he was already sad, scared, and hurting.* Aspen also avoided discussions with her mother to avoid the pain of bringing up negative memories. *We did not talk about her relationship with her husband, my father, who was abusive. I didn't talk about their relationship, because I didn't want to upset her more or confuse her, and honestly, I didn't want to relive any of the pain.*

Others felt a strong need to remain respectful to the Dying by not bringing up or saying something offensive. For instance, Zac noted that *I had to monitor the way I said things because I didn't want to say something the wrong way and offend or upset her.* Beth also shared that *on one hand I was trying not to be afraid to talk about any and all topics, but on the other hand, I really was afraid to upset my mom. At the same time, I realized that she may have wanted to cover the same subjects that I avoided, but I was too afraid of making other people in the room uncomfortable.* In the end, Beth played it safe and focused on more superficial topics but regretted it later.

Danielle struggled with the difficulty of knowing exactly the right thing to say; she didn't know what to talk about with the Dying. *The right thing to say was based on so many different things, both in her regard and in mine: religion, the characteristics of our relationship, or maybe simply what would have been most pleasant. There was a great deal of uncertainty in me, which may have been in part due to an uncertainty about my own identity, spiritually, and some uncertainty about who my aunt was on a deeper level.*

The struggle is real for many people, and you won't know what is okay or off-limits to talk about until you try to bring up some topics.

Begin with the easier ones and then go from there. Watch the Dying's responses and use their reactions to help guide your choices.

A Lack of Privacy

Kyra shared that she was aware during her talks that her grandmother had limited physical energy and that there were a lot of people that were also wanting to say goodbye. She told us *my grandmother had limited resources to share with several family members, not just me. So, my final conversation was short and public, and I felt like I was taxing her to make her talk. It was less of a dialogue and more of just things she wanted to say to me before she died.* When time is running short, sometimes the Living are limited by the circumstances and by the urgency of the needs of the Dying. Similarly, Evie shared that having other family members present during her interaction made her less open and forced her to keep some of her true feelings private. *I often feel embarrassed when I cry, and I had an audience—other family members—for the conversations; it was challenging with everyone watching and listening.* Evie makes an important observation: conversations are often very different if they happen in private, rather than in front of other family members or friends who may react to the information. Their examples illustrate the importance of trying to arrange private, one-on-one time between the Dying and the individual family members.

Suppressing Emotions

The end-of-life journey raises many emotions perceived as negative, such as sadness, fear, and anger, which are challenging to deal with. Two factors that explain the Living's hesitancy to display their emotions during their final conversations include family norms and personal expectations.

Family Norms. Do you come from a family that believes that every family member should be stoic, strong, and keep their emotions to themselves? Family norms run deep and have a great effect on how people display their emotions. If the family norm is to be stoic and to control emotions, then the Living may find these talks challenging. Curtis came from such a family. *My mother was a very stoic individual who did not cry. The way she was raised was that you do* *not show weakness and crying was a weakness.* Similarly, Tessa stated *that it was important for me to have emotional control. It's hard for me to control my feelings, while my mom was very strong in controlling hers, so I felt that I had to as well.* If the Dying has a history of keeping strong control over their feelings, then the Living typically want to mirror that behavior, no matter how difficult it might be. Cultural norms may also influence the family's expression of emotions. Fred explained *she was my mother, a German and very pragmatic. We never showed a lot of emotion at home, but we cared for each other even though we were not very expressive.* Fred's example illustrates that just because individuals do not express emotion, it does not mean that they are not experiencing the emotion internally and privately.

Personal Expectations. Whether to express negative emotions or not can come down to individuals' expectations of what is best for the situation. For instance, Amy stated that one of her goals during her conversation was to *not turn into a crying mess.* While Jerome explained, *I always tried not to cry and be strong.* For others, it was more of not wanting to cause the Dying any additional burden or sadness. Wallace explained that *seeing your loved one suffer and in pain is excruciating. His heart was failing, and he just looked terrible. It was not an easy sight to see, and I often excused myself from the room so I could compose myself again. I didn't want to add to his distress.* Indy's focus was on being a good partner to his father on his end-of-life journey. He stated that it was important to *allow my dad to talk and express his feelings about everything and being honest with him, without breaking down to the point where I can no longer help him in his journey.*

Cary's previous experience when his father was dying influenced his emotional expression. *Because of a previous bad experience with my father's death, I'm always afraid I'm going to say something that will send the Dying into an uncontrollable wailing mess! So, now when I am in similar circumstances, I am much more careful about controlling what I say and what emotions I show.*

Pressure of Time

Time frames how people enter their final conversations and determines what and how much is talked about during their interactions.

The first challenge pertaining to time is the stress experienced by the Living who didn't have enough time. Benjamin felt that *trying to fit 30 years of conversations, friendship, and memories into two hours is impossible.* We understand this stress, and Benjamin is right: two hours is not enough time, which is why we encourage the Living to begin these conversations sooner rather than later following a terminal diagnosis. Tianna rightfully noted that *the element of time constricts the breadth and depth of topics, especially when you are dealing with terminal illnesses.* And Max summed up his challenge when talking with his father after a lifetime of avoiding difficult conversations: *Trying to wrap up a lifetime of conversations in a short period was impossible. I had two weeks to be with him to talk, and it was difficult to get everything out after a lifetime of keeping everything in—my father was not one to have lengthy conversations. I had a lot of built-up hurt and uncertainty about our relationship, and it was not enough time to deal with it all.* We understand Max's frustration, and we encourage Max and others in similar constrained situations to recognize that any amount of time is better than no time at all. We do not believe that all our relational issues will be carried away with the Dying as they leave this earth, but taking the time to participate in final conversations can truly be a beginning point for personal healing.

Toby felt *a lot of pressure knowing that it could be my last conversation.* Similarly, Mara thought the biggest challenge was *knowing that the Dying is going to die soon, as if there's a time bomb about to go off any day instead of just unexpectedly dying.* We wonder, why is it that knowing that there is a terminal amount of time is seen as a time bomb that will explode while you are holding it? We hope that the Living come to the realization that if there is anything positive about knowing that there is a limited amount time left with the Dying, it is that the Living have time to say goodbye and anything else that needs to be said before time runs out. An unexpected death brings shock and no opportunity to say anything. Grief accompanies death whether there is time to say goodbye or not. Time to say goodbye . . . is a gift.

Health Barriers to Communication (Mental and Physical)

Hindrances to communicating with the Dying are not uncommon, and the Living may have few options if they are present. These barriers include mental deterioration from dementia and other medical conditions affecting communication at the end of life.

Dementia Impairments. Cognitive degeneration is more common than it used to be, in part because people are living longer than in past generations. Causes of dementia-related diseases include genetic factors, lifestyle choices (lack of exercise, stress, alcohol use, diet), and environmental influences that are still being explored. We know that if the Dying have some form of dementia, communication is negatively affected by the disease, making conversation challenging at best and impossible at worst. As Alonzo said, *When you deal with an individual with dementia, you lose them a little piece at a time, so by the time they leave you for good, you have already let them go in your mind. You hold on to the lucid conversations and the smiles and the hugs, because at the end, they don't talk to you anyway. But the smile when they see you says that inside of their mind, they know you and will always love you.* Alonzo learned to embrace whatever level of communication (verbal or nonverbal) that was possible with the Dying. If your loved one is suffering from these impairments, we want to encourage you to begin having final conversations with them sooner rather than later.

Maureen's father-in-law, David, died from Lewy body dementia, which impacted his mind and his body. David was a brilliant man, a history professor, and an author of multiple books. *Some family members began having final conversations with him once it was clear that he was suffering from some kind of dementia, as he still had lucid periods during the beginning and middle parts of his disease. Other family members had a more difficult time seeing this brilliant man change, so it was hard for them to interact with him at all, but everyone found some meaning, comfort, and closure when they finally participated in their own interactions with him.*

Kim shared the challenges that she had during her talks with her father, who had dementia. *He was rarely cognizant throughout his time in the hospital before his death. He was sort of stuck in a time loop that took him back to the Korean War and his experiences.* Kim shows us the frustration and loss that comes with interacting with the Dying when their disease had progressed so far. Barry chose to focus on the conversations that he had shared with his father prior to his diagnosis. *He died of Alzheimer's, so my most valued memories were before he had been officially diagnosed with the disease. We all saw the deterioration and his eventual death approaching.* Comfort and closure can definitely come from these earlier conversations. The early warning signs of Alzheimer's disease might be the signal that the Living need to begin having more frequent talks with their loved one, even prior to the official diagnosis, to get the most out of their interactions.

Unconsciousness and Other Physical Health Obstacles. There are times at the end of life when the final conversations are one-sided because the Dying are unconscious or have some other kind of medical obstacle that makes it impossible for them to talk with the Living. Some conversations may be entirely nonverbal and still be meaningful. Many medical professionals believe that individuals who are unconscious may be able to hear what the Living are saying to them and can feel when their hand is being held or their face is being stroked. Even if you never find out if this was the case with the Dying, you could still find some comfort and closure by saying what you need to say and by feeling their hand in yours. Eli felt the challenge of trying to have a conversation with one who is not conscious. *My grandma was in a coma when she and I had our final conversation, so I'm not sure if she heard me, but I hope so.*

Nora told us her husband *wasn't supposed to be able to speak because of the ventilator helping him breathe, but he grabbed it from his face just to tell me he loved me before anyone could stop him. That's something that I remember almost every day.* Nora knew that there are miracle moments that surprise us, have meaning for us, and stay with us for the rest of our lives. Margerie noted how physical pain can also act as a barrier to communication at the end of life. *His pain from the cancerous tumor in his cranium often made it impossible for him to talk about anything at all.* It is during these times that your presence and perhaps your touch may be all that you are able to give the Dying. With time and reflection these nonverbal acts of love and connection will become meaningful to the Living as well—you will be glad that you were there and that they were not alone.

Finally, Natalie recognized the value of observing that something was changing about her mother before there was a diagnosis. *We knew that things were bad for many months before the official diagnosis, so we had a chance to talk and iron out all of our issues before it was too late. Once she was diagnosed with terminal brain cancer, she was mostly unable to speak. It was me talking to her mostly, but if I hadn't gotten a chance to talk to her, I would have been devastated—if only because I wanted to reassure her that I would be okay, and she could let go.* Natalie realized what a gift it was to take the opportunity to talk with her mother when she saw the changes beginning. She also knew that the time spent with her following the progression of her disease, when her mother could no longer speak, was valuable and comforting for both.

Drawbacks of Technology

For better or worse, many of us have become accustomed to having personal conversations via social media. Sometimes the only way the Living could speak to the Dying was via FaceTime, Zoom, or Skype because of physical distance or medical restrictions. For instance, Jackson shared that *I lived far away in another state, so our conversations did not happen face-to-face, but happened over the phone or via other technology.* While this may not be ideal, technology has come a long way in a short period of time. The availability of cell phones ensures that people can contact each other more easily than we could in the era of landline phones. The newest technologies we have offer the opportunity to see the other person on the screen as well as hear their voice. Monica noted one major drawback to the use of technology for final conversations: *Since we only communicated through Skype and phone, the relationship didn't feel really as intimate as it should've been.* We agree with her. While technology may connect us in more ways than ever, it cannot support the same level of intimacy and connection that two people create when they are face-to-face with all of their senses engaged in the interaction.

Tianna agreed: *When my grandmother was sick, I was away at school. I often blame myself for not reaching out more in her final days. Most of our communication was via phone. I often replay the last hug in my head. I wasn't in a position to come home as often as I would have liked. I never got to actually see her in the hospital, just conversations over the phone.* Many family members live far away and may find themselves in a similar situation. If this is the case for you, there are a few things to keep in mind before you beat yourself up. The Dying may not want the Living to stop their lives—education or career—risking their future success. The Dying know that they are in your heart and mind every time they get a call or message from you. Remembering and replaying a last hug or kiss is a precious gift. Embrace it. Also know that some of the Dying truly prefer a smaller group of loved ones around them towards the end of their death journey. It is more peaceful and perhaps easier for them to let go of this earth and to let go of their loved ones.

Individual Challenges

The last set of obstacles to participating in final conversations are quite varied and are unique to each person's experience. For instance, Zane acknowledged that when his father was dying that he was *too young to make sense of the conversations.* Richard admitted that his *grief was too intense and overwhelming to actually engage in interactions with his mother.* We want to assure you that you can only do what you can do during the end-of-life journey. Participate in whatever talks you are capable of, then focus on whatever good memories you have of your loved one.

In other instances, the Dying did not reveal the seriousness of their illness until it was too late. As Bobbi described it, *I didn't have enough of them. The dire reality of my uncle's illness was not accurately expressed to us by him, and we were all shocked when he suddenly left, when we thought he was going to be fine. He made us feel like he was going to be just fine.* We wish this were not the case, but it happens more often than we can say. Please be compassionate and remember that this is their death journey and perhaps they are very private or they were coping with the news as best they could. One final conversation is better than none.

If you can accept your own challenges, it becomes possible to approach the Dying and participate in final conversations.

APPROACHING FINAL CONVERSATIONS

The impulse to approach final conversations is triggered when the reality of the death can no longer be denied and is finally accepted. Moving from denial to acceptance of the approaching death is a journey, and the amount of time it takes to get from one point to the next differs for everyone. Austin said that the hardest thing to do to get to acceptance was *getting over the grim reaper in the room.* The use of his language "the grim reaper" demonstrates the negative view that many people have about death. It is a boogeyman, a dark force stealing someone away from us. However, it is a natural part of the life cycle, even if for some it is a much shorter life cycle than for others. Austin continued, *I have now participated in other final conversations and talks about death, and I can say that dealing with the issues—getting over the grim reaper—with my mom when I was 15, made it possible for me to deal well with any conversation about death.* Austin demonstrated that his experience of final conversations helped him become more comfortable and willing to participate in these talks. As with any communication, it is a skill that can be learned and improved.

Shawn's approach to final conversations came from her *knowing that I only had a limited amount of time with her. She had been such a powerful force in my life, and I was coming to the realization that she was no longer going to be there, so I had to take advantage of whatever time we had left together.*

There are also some people like Harry who did not want to talk with his father about dying. *He knew it, I knew it, but we didn't say it. We talked around it.* While both the Dying and the Living may accept the death prognosis, they may still choose not to talk about it and talk as if nothing has changed. While we don't recommend this approach, keep in mind that the Living and Dying can have beneficial final conversations *without* talking about death and dying. If you recall, "death and dying" is not one of the six themes of final conversations that emerged from our research reported earlier in this book. At the same time, approaching communication at the end of life in this way may have several negative consequences. The Dying may feel very alone during their death journey if they cannot share their thoughts and feelings with close loved ones. The Living may miss out on an opportunity to learn more about the Dying and themselves. Finally, the Living may not have the benefit of the Dying's help in preparing them for a life without them.

SUMMARY

Avoiding final conversations or particular topics in them is not a surprising reaction if we view death and dying negatively and encounter obstacles to communication with the Dying. Some of the obstacles discussed can be easily overcome, such as making sure that everyone gets some alone time and privacy for their conversations. Working through expectations and norms regarding the expression of emotions during these interactions at the end of life is a bigger challenge. It takes some negotiation; you may need to take a risk to be your authentic self. Following a terminal diagnosis, time is almost always going to feel like pressure, which means that beginning your final conversations sooner rather than later is the best response to this challenge. Awareness about the specific disease symptoms and complications that may affect the Dying's communication over time should motivate you to have the conversations as soon as possible. Living at a distance is going to require you to plan a trip to spend time with the Dying when possible, and when those times are not possible, technology allows family members to connect as often as you want—just be sure to do it. Finally, there are some personal challenges that you may not be able to control. Work through what you can and, as for the rest, let go and remind yourself that you did the best that you could at that time.

Avoiding and approaching final conversations are opposing forces that must be negotiated within ourselves and with those we love during the death journey. The big takeaway from this chapter is that final conversations may not be easy, but the most fulfilling things in life are often not easy. It is in the effort—the overcoming of uncertainty, fear, and obstacles—where people grow, learn, and find meaning in life.

TIPS FOR BETTER CONVERSATIONS

- You may want to consider writing some notes about topics you want to remember to talk about with the Dying. During the sometimes chaotic and often emotional circumstances surrounding the end-of-life journey, we can forget what we want to ask or say.
- Try to give family members and close friends opportunities to have alone time with the Dying. Whether the communication is verbal or nonverbal, final conversations are different one-on-one than they are when many people are present or when using technology.
- Trust your intuition as to whether it is safe for you to be truly honest and exposed. Only *you* know your history with the Dying, and you need to make this personal decision yourself.
- No matter how challenging and difficult it is, make yourself present, vulnerable, and open to authentic conversation.
- Resist speaking in unrealistically positive or future-oriented ways, which may shut down what the Dying wants to really talk about.
- Allow the Dying to talk of death. Try not to shut them down by denying their talk of dying in order to alleviate your own discomfort about talking about death.

chapter 16

You Can Too: Communication Skills for the Last Day and Every Day

I've experienced death in two ways: Death with an understanding that the end was near, with plenty of time for final conversations. And then an unexpected death with so many things left unspoken. This is why I say to everyone, if you're given the gift of a final conversation, take it, because that's what it is—a gift—*one that isn't given to everyone.* (Carissa)

Like fingerprints, no two final conversations are the same. Some are uplifting, beautiful, exhilarating, and life-changing; others are sad, frustrating, mundane, or gut-wrenching. No single interaction will fulfill your every expectation, but after some time and reflection, each adds to what can be gained overall from them, and will deliver unexpected gifts. Your final conversation is unique because it is created by you and your dying loved one, making it irreplaceable.

We have spent most of our lives teaching young adults about interpersonal communication: what it is, how it develops, who you choose to relate to, when you can expect communication challenges, why it is easy to communicate with some people and not with others, and which patterns succeed and which fail. Still, even though we can make educated guesses about communication in relationships, we can never predict for sure what will happen in any particular conversation. As humans, we are unpredictable, and communicate in the moment based on all our prior experiences. No one person's experiences match another's completely, so our communication choices vary greatly. You've probably had the experience of anticipating an important conversation and planning out everything you wanted to say. Yet, when the conversation began, you faced a real, live person who reacted, interrupted, cried, or asked questions, and foiled your well-rehearsed plan altogether. You likely never got to say half of what you had planned. How you respond during an interaction arises from multiple factors, and every person has the potential to respond differently on any given day, depending on the circumstances of that conversation.

Of course, as you get to know someone, you find it easier to predict how he or she will respond to you. But whenever you get two people together to truly connect—exchange and listen to each other deeply—something new is created: a relationship in which to learn and grow. That is why final conversations can be life changing. If ever you are going to be true to yourself and, at the same time, deeply concerned with your loved one, here is the last opportunity to do it. We want to prepare you for that interaction in the hope that you will have a more satisfying conversation with the Dying. But we also hope you carry the skills into your other relationships. We will walk you through why you should participate in final conversations, how to prepare for them, how to listen, what you might want to say, and when to ask for help.

WHY ENGAGE IN FINAL CONVERSATIONS?

First, there's the altruistic side: Giving your time and company to the Dying reflects an understanding that you want to be there with them at their end of life. The Dying often do want to talk—about death itself, about preparations with which they need help, or about how much they will miss you and life. If you can be the person who allows them to talk freely without fear of causing you pain or discomfort, then you will have no regrets. Second, which might be considered the selfish side: receiving the gifts of final conversations is all about you. All motivations to communicate can be perceived as "selfish," in the sense that you benefit in some way from the interaction, and so does the person you're talking to. In the case of last interactions, the gifts to the Dying will ease their passing; the gifts to the Living will be realized with time in terms of maturity and capacity to live fully even in the midst of grief.

Both tangible and intangible rewards keep the memories vivid and may expand your view of your place and purpose in this life. Many of you will receive memorable messages of love and caring that make you feel valued and worthwhile. Some of you will find resolution to difficult or challenging relationships and subsequent peace of mind. You may experience a confirmation of your worth or perhaps even a shift in your spiritual beliefs from your final conversations. Most of you will learn to live with greater joy, and some will find your self-image shift in a positive way. These kinds of personal growth can lead you to change your life's purpose and path or give you the resolve you need to stay your course in life.

Remember: it is often the things that we *don't do* that we regret later. The Living told us overwhelmingly that they are glad that they had their final conversations and that they would do it again given the opportunity. If you are willing to take the chance to grow and to be open to what might happen, then please read on for suggestions on how to do it in the best way possible. Please take our advice according to what feels right for you and for your unique situation, but remember that doing something for the first time always causes some uneasiness. Our advice is based on what we have been privileged to learn from the Living from two decades of research on this topic, and on our combined 65 years of teaching interpersonal communication to thousands of students.

HOW TO PREPARE FOR FINAL CONVERSATIONS

As we were told by the Living, don't set too many expectations for how you think it will go. Just be ready to listen carefully and to follow your interaction where it leads you. We'll show you a few skills you can practice to make that more likely. But first, set the stage.

Your Availability

If you know your loved one has a terminal diagnosis, begin by looking into the optimal amount of time you can put aside to spend with the Dying. Check with your boss, family, and friends to see how they can help you free yourself from daily responsibilities to make time to spend with your loved one.

Timing Your Visit

Once your availability is opened up, figure out the best possible time for the Dying to engage with you. Talking sooner rather than later is encouraged. The sooner the interactions begin, the more you may be able to share with the Dying. The closer the Dying is to their death, the less likely it is that they can interact and talk with you.

You will want to ask the primary caregiver, the medical practitioners, or the hospice workers about the best time to talk with the Dying. For example, if it's likely that the Dying will sleep immediately after pain medication is administered, then that time should be ruled out. Find out when the Dying is most alert and able to focus. But if you get there and the Dying is not awake, be flexible. The caregivers can give you their best guess of when to visit, but the days and nights of the Dying become less predictable as the end nears.

Choosing the Place

The surroundings can make a world of difference in the nature and tone of the conversation. Do the two of you have a favorite place? This could be somewhere simple and easy to get to, such as a backyard patio, a garden, or somewhere a short drive away that holds special meaning for the two of you. You may not have the choice to go somewhere other than the Dying's room, but it is something to think about if it is an option. People tend to open up and talk when they are in a familiar and comfortable place—this is true for both the Dying and the Living. Take advantage of the time that is afforded you, and the available places that make both of you relaxed and happy.

Privacy

Consider the physical location and think about how it will work for a private talk. If it is a home, who else visits and when? Is there a door that can be closed? If it is a hospital, is it a shared room? How noisy is it? When are the visiting hours? How many people are likely to come and at which times? Privacy is not necessary, but it often makes a difference. People self-disclose and share more openly when they feel safe and there is privacy.

Frequency and Duration

Make sure that you arrive on time and go as often as is allowed. There are gatekeepers at the end of life, and it will be their job to limit the amount of interaction that the Dying has with others. The Dying may have requested limited access, and you have to respect their wishes—this is their time. It is an honor and a privilege to be given space and time with the Dying; treat it as such. You may need to keep your visits brief—take your cues from the Dying and from the caregivers.

The Caregiver's Role

The primary gatekeeper may also be the primary caregiver. That role gives them more rights than someone who is only visiting. Try to honor that person's rights as well. The primary caregiver may be exhausted and seem unreasonable. Be compassionate and see if there is anything that you can do to help the caregiver—perhaps they can go out for a break while you have a visit with the Dying. They are usually very aware of the Dying's capability on any given day or hour. You never know what the Dying has asked the caregiver to say or do—perhaps even to be the "heavy" in the situation. Here is where it is important to think about your relationship with the Dying and the caregiver to make some sense out of the requests or restrictions being presented to you. Using a calm tone and nonthreatening language, ask the caregiver direct questions about the situation. You could ask, "I want to see mom more often, but my efforts are being blocked. Is there something that I need to be aware of, or something that I can do to help?" If they seem unreasonable, then try to get some insight from a third party on how to get more time and access to the Dying. You may also want to consider your own behavior. Are you helping the situation or are you causing more tension in the environment?

Limitations

One more thing you must ask the caregivers is if there will be any limitations to interacting. That possibility increases as time toward death nears. Can the Dying still hear and speak? Does the Dying recognize people? What kind of touch is okay, and what kind may cause discomfort? Armed with this information, you can feel well prepared to meet the needs of the Dying and to engage as best you can. Later in this chapter, we give details on how to handle such limitations.

HOW TO COMMUNICATE WITH SKILL

There are two halves to communication: listening and speaking. Sometimes the parts are out of balance. Most people are natural speakers. But listening is a different matter. Unless you have a driving interest in hearing what another has to say, you often tune out all but what you expect to hear. Listening is a critical skill in all interactions, but it is absolutely necessary when you interact with your loved one who may be talking with you for the last time. We recommend that you practice this skill first with other people who are important to you. It cannot hurt, and you will be more comfortable with the skills by the time you really must have them. Go ahead and share what you are doing with your practice partners. They may be thrilled with the extra attention, and you may hear something you never would have expected.

But you may say, "I'm in the process of saying goodbye now; I don't have time to practice." Or "My life is too busy; I don't have time to learn new skills." If you feel that you cannot practice, at least read through this list, so you are more aware of these skills. A few of them need no practice at all. But ask yourself if you feel prepared or not. Most of the Living who contributed their stories had no special training. Your own good sense will serve you. If you have time to practice, these skills can help you feel more prepared and gain more from the experience.

Listening

Give Yourself a Reason to Listen Carefully. Hearing is different from listening. Hearing is a physical sense; listening is a cognitive act. Listening is a conscious choice and an active process. Words can just amount to background noise if you aren't truly paying attention. Go in with an open mind and heart. Let the Dying say what they need to say and fully listen to them; try not to interrupt them. Some of the meaning or impact of what they are saying to you may not emerge until days or weeks later.

Be Other-Centered. When you focus on what the other person needs and wants in a conversation instead of being focused on yourself, conversations often go better. Communication at its best is like a mirror. If you treat your partner as you would like to be treated, listened to, responded to, then your partner often responds in kind.

Stop Talking. Yes, this one seems obvious, but humans love the sound of their own voices. Once you have a reason to listen—and practice will reinforce your success—try to get comfortable with silence. After you have exchanged greetings and pleasantries, stop talking and see what develops. Imagine that you will be relating this talk to someone later on and that you need to remember what was said. Then stretch your memory by jotting down a few notes after your conversation.

Get Out of Your Own Head. Are you really listening or are you preoccupied thinking about what you want to say next? Be careful, you may miss out on something precious and important because you are distracted by your own thoughts. Are you becoming defensive and thinking about ways to argue with the Dying about one point or another? Being "right" is not important. When you are "right," someone you love is "wrong," and then your relationship suffers. Instead, clear your head of the distractions created by fear and the need to be right.

Speaking

Ask a Question. If you've allowed a silence and the Dying hasn't spoken, you might try a question. But do allow a decent silence. Count to at least 20. Meanwhile, smile, make eye contact, hold a hand, act friendly and interested. If it seems right, you can start with simple questions that require little effort such as "How are they treating you here?" or "Can I do anything for you?" Then move to *open-ended* questions that allow the Dying to talk for a while and perhaps move to the topics they want to pursue. For example, you could ask, "What have you been thinking about lately?" or even specific requests such as "Can you tell me again how you and Aunt Jean met?" These kinds of questions not only show an interest in hearing what the Dying has to say but give the Dying the chance to talk at length and thus get to a topic of importance to you both.

If you ask only *closed-ended* questions such as "Are you too cold with that window open?" you will likely get only one-word replies that lead nowhere. However, if the answers to your open questions remain brief, you may want to go a bit deeper. But again, leave your questions open so the Dying has some choice about how to respond. An example would be: "Is there anything in particular you'd like to talk about?" The Dying may just want to reminisce about old times. On the other hand, they may want to talk about their thoughts about death. Sometimes the Dying give you hints; at other times you will get no such help. If your relationship is good, you can be fairly direct if you suspect a need. Sam was able to say bluntly to his mother, *"Do you want to talk about dying?"* and she immediately jumped in and started talking with her son about her thoughts and fears (in Chapter 13). At the same time, if you ask and the Dying changes the subject or looks uncomfortable, then let it go. Try not to pressure the Dying into a conversation that they don't want.

Paraphrase Your Loved One's Statement. The paraphrase is the hallmark of good listening. To paraphrase is to say in your own words what your partner has just told you. You are not mimicking them, but rather demonstrating your understanding of what they said and felt. Paraphrasing not only lets the speaker know that they have been heard, but helps the listener clarify their understanding and remember the gist of what has been said.

For example, let's say your mother has just told you: "I'm afraid it's going to hurt." If you repeat that exactly, word for word, she may wonder what is wrong or if you are making fun of her. But if you said instead, "So, you're afraid that death will be painful." If it wasn't what she meant, she could clarify her meaning. For example, "No, I don't think it will physically hurt to die. I'm afraid it will hurt too much to leave you." Paraphrasing is really an opportunity to let the other person feel understood.

Again, practice this with friends. You might feel awkward at first, but you'll find it really helps your ability to focus on people and understand them. The more that you use this communication skill, the easier it becomes. As a bonus, your partners will appreciate being understood. Be careful to only paraphrase statements that you want to be sure that you understood what the other person was saying, or else you risk annoying the other person and slowing down the conversation too much.

Do Perception Checks. You may not need to do this in every interaction, but it can be particularly helpful in difficult relationships. Communication can be so ambiguous that misunderstandings arise. A perception check is simply giving the other person two choices regarding your interpretation of the message. For instance, "You just told me that you are afraid. Are you afraid of dying or are you afraid of being in pain?" By giving two choices (even if both are wrong) you are telling the other person that you want to truly understand and not misunderstand the message. Be careful not to do this all the time, because if it is overused, it can become frustrating. Perception checking is best used when there is some potential for confusion and where clarification is needed.

Say What You Feel. Over and over, the Living said: *"Say what you feel . . . don't leave anything unsaid."* Leave the door open for the Dying to express their feelings, but also allow yourself the opportunity to speak your mind and heart as well.

In a *difficult relationship,* this may mean putting tough topics on the table, allowing the Dying to speak, and then allowing yourself a say. At the same time, the Living taught us that they realized that the end of life is not the time to hurt the Dying (in Chapter 9). They found a way to talk with the Dying and to say what they needed to say without threatening, accusing, or insulting the Dying. All of the Living in this group who had difficult relationships with the Dying stressed that they wanted to express their thoughts and feelings to the Dying as a path to begin their healing.

In an *easy relationship*, simply expressing what is felt at the time will serve. For example: "I'm feeling at a loss to know what to do" or "I love you so much and will miss you forever." When the Dying is unable to speak, there is an opening for the Living to simply express what they feel. Remember that you can also use nonverbal communication to express what you are feeling as well. A touch can express at times what is too difficult to say in words.

Being Silent

Pay Attention to Nonverbal Communication. Watch the Dying's nonverbal communication. It is amazing what can be observed if you listen with your eyes as well as ears. With an increase in awareness about nonverbal communication you will see more and more as you practice this skill—and it is a skill. Believe it or not, you are probably already an expert regarding the nonverbal communication of those closest to you.

Be There. There will come a time when all has been said and done; all that is left to do is to be present in the moment. If both the Dying and the Living are at peace with everything that has been said and done, then merely being there is what is required. Being there can include hugs, kisses, caresses, deep eye contact . . . all the many ways we have to express our caring and closeness without talking. Playing music, reading poetry, watching a meaningful movie . . . all these pastimes can constitute being there too. What is chosen is limited only by your imagination and the physical comfort of the Dying.

WHEN TO ASK FOR HELP

Sometimes you may have to rely on professionals. When you are walking alongside the Dying, you will probably have to consult medical personnel and caregivers. You may need suggestions about how to communicate with the Dying whose communication abilities are diminished. And when your loved one is gone—or even before—you may also wish to contact a grief counselor.

Medical and Caregiving Professionals

You will find that the Dying's doctors, nurses, social workers, and chaplains have a lot of information about the Dying that can help you have the best interaction possible. They look busy, and they are. But don't let that stop you from trying to find out about the Dying's physical strength, medical regimen, or daily routine. When they have a minute, explain who you are and why you are asking—that you want to maximize your last interactions with the Dying. If you are not a family member, doctors will be reluctant to speak to you about some aspects of the Dying's medical status. Indeed, there are confidentiality rules that prevent them from giving you specific information.

Despite legalities, you may ask about *the basics*: When is the Dying most likely to be alert and pain-free? Is it okay to touch and hug her? When is the best time to have a private conversation with him? The answers should be sufficient to give you the best chance to optimize your interactions.

Caregivers' services run the gamut from simple assistance with grooming and feeding to highly specialized nursing or end-of-life care. If the Dying has in-home care, that professional may be a nurse who can also answer the medical questions listed above as well as those that are more about general care and nurturing. You should ask about this especially if you want to do *something special* for the Dying. For example, if Dad always had sore feet and you occasionally gave him footbaths and pedicures, you may want to follow your impulse to share that closeness again, yet you do not want to interfere with the caregiver's duties. So, ask the caregiver if it would be appropriate for you to perform this duty while she does other tasks. Remember to ask if there is any possible danger to the Dying with this or any other comforting ritual you'd like to give.

Other questions become more pertinent as death approaches, such as "Can she still hear me?" or "Is he in pain?" Those who work with the Dying suspect that hearing is often the last sense still active in the final stages of the dying process. Therefore, they encourage you to continue talking, even when it seems the Dying cannot hear. Go ahead. You will feel some closure and there's a good chance that your words could comfort the Dying and assist them to cross over without fear.

Be sensitive to the possibility that even the unresponsive Dying may want some peace and quiet. Say what you need to but be wary of chattering. Present a *calming presence*. For instance, when Maureen's mother was in a coma, there were many family members in the room surrounding her and quietly talking amongst themselves, around her and in her space. Someone in the room looked around and suggested that Pat may need some quiet. Maureen remembers looking up as she and the others were walking out of the room, and Pat slightly nodded her head yes—a small movement, but unmistakable. She did need it to be quiet and peaceful. Everyone made sure that the house was calm and quiet, with only one person at a time holding vigil by her side for the remaining 38 hours of her life.

Limitations: Interaction When the Dying's Senses Are Impaired

Some of you will want to talk with Dying who have become limited in their communication abilities. They may not be able to speak (e.g., paralysis, throat cancer, brain tumor), or to hear (e.g., advanced age, disease), or to respond normally (e.g., Alzheimer's disease, coma). What can you do in this case? We can give you some general suggestions, but your best bet again is to consult with the medical professionals. They know the extent of the impairment and the range of possible adaptations you could try.

For example, if you know that Aunt Rae's *hearing* has deteriorated, we suggest that you talk in short sentences, and a bit slower, clearer, and louder. She may be able to hear you well enough as long as background noise is minimal, and you articulate your words well. If you are tempted to shout, stop. Shouting can be perceived as a sign of anger, so it is not an effective remedy for hearing difficulties.

Pain may be a constant companion to the Dying. If you've ever had a really bad toothache or hurt after surgery, you know it's difficult to think straight, never mind carry on a calm, intimate conversation. The right pain medication makes a world of difference for those with limited time remaining to them. It can mean the difference between having a long, heartfelt talk and an abbreviated one punctuated by gasps of pain. The professionals attending the Dying will know when they experience their pain-free peak, when the medication is beginning to fail, and when it's just best to "be there" if the pain cannot be allayed.

Finally, some of the Dying are *unresponsive*. Many health care professionals believe that even those in a coma can be reached, that they can still take in information even if they don't respond. So, don't give up and walk away if the Dying is unresponsive and in a coma. Although you may never know for sure, you can still express what you need to through words and through touch. Do it for yourself, and you just may be doing it for the Dying as well.

Getting Through the Grief

It is almost impossible to grasp the gifts that come from final conversations if you are buried in grief. Losing someone whom you love hurts, and there will be grief whether you have those last interactions or not. However, we were told by the Living that having final conversations helped them to deal with their grief and bereavement more effectively. But it is not a cure-all. With death, many feel that grief is inevitable and simply must be endured. To some extent this is true. Grief is inevitable, but *how long* must it be endured? Grief can be intense, and it can come and go for years. But it does come and go; life does continue. When grief becomes depression and lasts more than a year, it becomes a constant and damaging companion.

What if you just can't go on? What if the grief of losing your dearest friend, your spouse, your child is just debilitating? What if it isn't just you? What if, after your spouse's death, your children didn't talk to anyone, they withdrew, their grades deteriorated, their friendships withered? If you are just too sad to make them talk about it, don't suffer, and don't let them suffer. There are people—some of them shared their personal experiences with us in this book—who specialize in grief counseling. It's what they know; it's what they've experienced; it's why they have great compassion for the grieving. They have been well trained and often work with hospice facilities. Seek them out and use their expertise. They work so that you can feel whatever you need to feel, and then to come back into the brilliant light of a full life.

The gifts of final conversations will return to the Living in waves—waves of memories, waves of inspiration, and waves of love—but only if the Living can dig themselves out from their depths of grief. These waves can last for years, perhaps forever. Some of the Living who talked with us recalled their last words from long ago. For Roy it was 27 years after the death of his mother, and he still recalled his conversation vividly and fondly. Words, gazes, touches live on long after the Dying are gone.

SUMMARY

Although there is no "ideal" final conversation, some are more fulfilling than others. Many of the Living trusted their intuition to find the right communication skills. You do not have to guess or to fear failure. You can prepare and practice.

Preparation includes setting aside time, finding the right time and place for private visits with the Dying, and following through with the visits in respect of the Dying's preferences.

Your communication skills may meet your needs for everyday tasks, yet you find your confidence dwindling as you approach your last interactions with your loved one. We urge you to practice being a good communicator: know how to listen well, when to speak, and when to be silent. We know, from years of teaching these skills, that they can become second nature with practice.

If you are currently in the midst of accompanying a loved one on their death journey and you don't have the time or energy to practice the communication skills, then realize that you have already become more aware of them by reading this book and by reading the Livings' stories. Go ahead and go for it! The time spent with the Dying will be better than you think; you will be better than you give yourself credit for.

Know when to seek help. You will be more comfortable with last interactions if you know what to expect about the Dying's communication capacities. Finally, take care of yourself. You cannot receive all that is possible from final conversations if you are paralyzed by grief, exhaustion, or fear. Get the support you need to walk back into your full and beautiful life.

The most important thing to remember is this: Showing up is a large part of success. Although you may want to say and hear profound messages, the fact that you are there is often more important to the Dying than what you say and how you say it.

Be there. Listen. Love.
Be grateful for the opportunity to have a good goodbye.

ABOUT THE AUTHORS

Maureen Keeley has been a Professor at Texas State University (TXST) for the past 30 years. For almost four decades, she has been teaching, researching, and writing about the verbal and nonverbal communication in family and close relationships, with a goal of improving peoples' lives and relationships. Twenty-six years ago, Maureen's mom was dying from cancer and, while her family and she surrounded her with love and care at the end of her life, they weren't sure how to talk with her or what they wanted her to say to them. Maureen went looking for answers and found nothing, because no one had asked family members about their conversations with their dying loved ones, so researching communication at the end of life became her life's work. Specifically, she has focused on communication at the end of life between family members and their loved ones who are terminally ill. In addition to her co-authored book, *Final Conversations*, with Julie Yingling in 2007, she has published dozens of research articles and book chapters; as well as given numerous workshops and presentations on the topic. When her dad died a few years ago, she and her family were now very comfortable with how to talk with him, leaving nothing left unsaid. Maureen lives with her husband, Mark, and their dog, Boo, in Central Texas, and they have two grown children, Ian and Meagan, who live nearby. When not teaching or writing, she loves spending time with her friends and family, talking and laughing under her pergola.

Julie Yingling is a writer, painter, gardener, and professor emerita from Cal Poly Humboldt. For 25 years, she taught, researched, and wrote about children's communication and interaction across the lifespan. As an academic, she published research articles, texts, and book chapters. Near the end of Julie's career, Maureen wanted a partner on a passion project and asked her to collaborate on exploring people's conversations with dying loved ones. Julie missed the opportunity to be with her father when he died because she couldn't get to him in time when weather delayed her flight. This project gave her the opportunity to reflect on all the correspondence and visits they shared during his last year of life. After some consideration, Julie realized that she had the opportunity to continue her life's work by now exploring the other end of the life spectrum—the communication during the shutting down of life rather than the growing up. As they worked together to understand the information from their first set of interviews, they found they collaborated well and enjoyed each other's company. So, when Maureen asked her again in 2022 to co-author the book that would express all they knew about the good goodbye, she agreed happily. After living and working in Colorado, Wisconsin, Iowa, and California, she returned after retiring to Rhode Island where she spent her childhood. And she cherished the gift of being with her mother at the end of her life in 2010. She lives in the woods with her spouse, Rick, and dog, Ziggy.

Hay House Titles of Related Interest

YOU CAN HEAL YOUR LIFE, the movie,
starring Louise Hay & Friends
(available as an online streaming video)
www.hayhouse.com/louise-movie

THE SHIFT, the movie,
starring Dr. Wayne W. Dyer
(available as an online streaming video)
www.hayhouse.com/the-shift-movie

***

THE TOP FIVE REGRETS OF THE DYING: A Life Transformed by the Dearly Departing, by Bronnie Ware

LOVE NEVER DIES: How to Reconnect and Make Peace with the Deceased, by Dr. Jamie Turndorf

YOU CAN HEAL YOUR HEART: Finding Peace After a Breakup, Divorce, or Death, by Louise Hay and David Kessler

VISIONS, TRIPS, AND CROWDED ROOMS: Who and What You See Before You Die, by David Kessler

All of the above are available at your local bookstore, or may be ordered by contacting Hay House (see next page).

***

We hope you enjoyed this Hay House book. If you'd like to receive our online catalog featuring additional information on Hay House books and products, or if you'd like to find out more about the Hay Foundation, please contact:

Hay House Publishers (India) Pvt Ltd
Muskaan Complex, Plot No. 3,
B-2, Vasant Kunj, New Delhi 110 070
Phone: +91 11 41761620
www.hayhouse.co.in

—

Published in the United States by:
Hay House LLC, P.O. Box 5100, Carlsbad, CA 92018-5100
(760) 31-7695 or (800) 654-5126
www.hayhouse.com® • www.hayfoundation.org

Published in Australia by:
Hay House Australia Publishing Pty Ltd
18/36 Ralph St., Alexandria NSW 2015
Phone: +61 (02) 9669 4299
www.hayhouse.com.au

Published in the United Kingdom by:
Hay House UK Ltd
1st Floor, Crawford Corner,
91–93 Baker Street, London W1U 6QQ
Phone: +44 (0)20 3927 7290
www.hayhouse.co.uk

—